Pauev an.
GTC CHESTR
.99

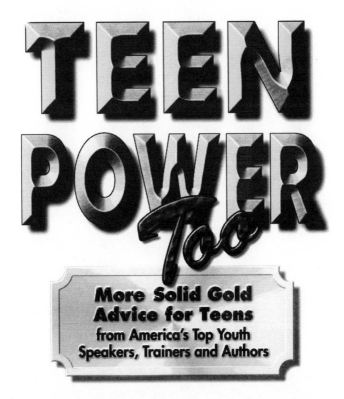

TEEN POWER Too

More Solid Gold Advice for Teens
from America's Top Youth Speakers, Trainers and Authors

JeVon Thompson • Eric Chester • Ellen Marie
Bobby Petrocelli • Julie Evans • Bill Cordes
Bob Lenz • Dr. Lewis Dodley • Micah Jacobson
Ed Gerety • Susie Vanderlip • Patrick T. Grady
and C. Kevin Wanzer

Compiled by
Eric Chester

Printed by Patterson Printing, Benton Harbor, Michigan

Cover design and layout by Ad Graphics, Tulsa, Oklahoma
(800) 368-6196

Library of Congress Catalog Card Number: 97-065414

ISBN: 0-9651447-1-2

TEEN POWER™
& TEEN POWER TOO™
are registered trademarks of ChesPress Publications

Published by:

ChesPress Publications
a subsidiary of Chester Performance Systems
1410 Vance St., Suite 201
Lakewood, CO 80215
(303)239-9999

Additional copies of
TEEN POWER TOO
can be obtained from any of the authors.
Contact information is at the end of the book.

Quantity discounts are available.

Contents

Where the authors are from, by chapter number

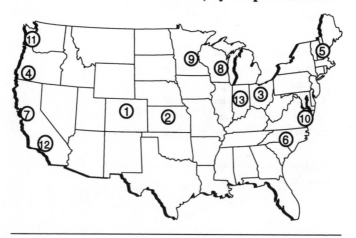

Too read, or not too read?

That is always the question when you open the cover of a new book. Take this one for example. You haven't even made it to an actual chapter and already there's this voice going off inside of you saying things like; *"Why should I read this?"* *"Where are the cool pictures of neat stuff?"* *"Who are all of these people, and why did each of 'em only write one chapter?"* *"Am I gonna get class credit for reading this?"* *"Why am I talking to myself?"* *"Would this paper taste good?"* *"Are the answers to my math homework listed in the back?"*

Instead of asking yourself *"Why should I read this?"* you should be asking *"Why shouldn't I?"* You've already taken a step in the right direction by reading this far. Don't stop now – you are on a roll. Keep reading; this is simply TOO cool to put on the shelf.

You see, if this were the kind of book that was written by only one person, you'd be getting only one perspective. But this book is a joint effort of thirteen authors; and if two heads are better than one, imagine how powerful a book can be that contains the perspective of thirteen different people, each of whom captured their best 'stuff' in 2,500 words or less!

Don't get locked-in to reading this from front to back. Each chapter is a mini 'stand alone' book of its own, so skip around! Pick a chapter that looks interesting, and dive in. Then go to the "Who Wrote What and Why" section and read the profile of the author. If you feel like it, contact them and give 'em your feedback. Now when was the last time a book gave you these kind of options?

Too read or not too read? That may be the question – but only you have the answer. Enjoy!

Eric Chester

Bed Bugs,
The Boogie Man,
and Other Myths

by
ERIC CHESTER

**TEEN
POWER
Too**

Bed Bugs, The Boogie Man, *and Other Myths*

by
ERIC CHESTER

"Whaddayamean there's no such thing as the Easter Bunny?"

I remember that gloomy afternoon when my mom broke the horrifying news to me. I was devastated. I felt my whole world cave in. I had grown up loving the Easter Bunny and held the hope of one day meeting him face to face. Now my dream was over! Mom just stood there motionless, as if she didn't care how deeply I was hurt. She appeared unusually cold and callous, insensitive to my suffering.

There was nothing left for me to say or do. So I grabbed my keys and coat and left to pick up my son from soccer practice.

At some point, we all discover much of what we were told growing up just isn't true. I've had to face the fact that there is no Easter Bunny. And I've got a hunch that Big Bird isn't really a bird at all, but a human inside a costume!

Concoctions, white lies, and distortions fill our childhood scrapbook. A lot of this stuff is just plain silly and has probably been passed down from some kind of gullible ancient civilization. But that didn't stop it from coming through your front door, did it? Growing up, you've undoubtedly heard (and perhaps even believed) these timeless beauties:

> *"Eat your vegetables, they'll put hair on your chest."*
> *"This spanking will hurt me more than it will hurt you."*
> *"Don't cross your eyes - they may stick like that forever."*
> *"Santa knows if you've been bad or good."*
> *"If you swallow a watermelon seed, it will grow in your stomach."*
> *"When I was your age, I walked eight miles to school in waist high snow...."*

These are just a few of the "myths of adolescence," and for the most part, they can be dismissed as harmless. But not all the myths are easy to spot, and some are rather dangerous.

As a parent, I'm guilty of being a myth maker. However, I've recently become a "myth breaker"; helping my kids separate truth from the fictional stories, lines, and statements they hear every day.

I've got a house full of teens; 3.89 of them, to be exact. (My youngest is only 11, but she thinks she's eleventeen.) Their choices will determine their future, and I want them to base those choices on the truth. Here are some of the more dangerous myths that have crept into their lives.

Myth #23 – The only way to "fit in" is to be like the others.

No one can make my day like Holli. She's a 16-year-old junior with a killer smile and thick, wavy hair that could star in its own Pantene® commercial. You can't get on her bad side; she doesn't have one. Holli finds the good in everyone.

Even though she hangs with a popular crowd, Holli is struggling to fit in. I know she's smart enough to make good decisions, but lately, the pressure of trying to fit in with her friends has caused her to do some pretty dumb things, getting her into some pretty messy situations with some pretty harsh consequences.

I know the road Holli is traveling all too well. During my teens, I was forever on the outside, looking in. Since I wasn't a very good athlete or a popular guy, the only thing I felt I had to offer the "ins" was to be their primary source of school comedy. No, I wasn't trying to be the class clown. That position was already taken by Marty Stone, who was as "in" as a kid could get. Instead, I became his first assistant, or as my dad often called me, "Marty's puppet."

Marty had a warped mind. I, like everyone else, thought Marty was hysterical. Unlike everyone else, I'd volunteer to act out his warped pranks. Marty would merely dream up a scheme, stunt, or gag – and I'd do it! I remember him coaxing me into soaking the bottoms of my tennis shoes with yellow paint and walking through the central lobby of our high school. Another time he had me shake up a can of Pepsi, pull the top, and toss it into the middle of the gym floor during a pep rally. But the ultimate stunt occurred when he goaded me into streaking (running naked) through cheerleader tryouts. (I didn't even make the squad.) Numerous stunts and gags, always the same result: Marty got the credit and I got the unscheduled school vacations (suspensions).

Looking back, I now understand that my continual efforts to become popular and gain acceptance from those I viewed as "in" worked against me. Every time I changed my behaviors and attitudes to fit in, I actually lost a little more of myself. However, when I acted in accordance with who I really was, ignoring the prompting and pressures of Marty and those like him, I found myself in the company of people who really liked me for who and what I was. Granted, it was a smaller, less-flashy crowd, but those friendships were genuine and unconditional.

So you're probably thinking that I learned my lesson and stopped trying to fit in after high school, right? Nope. Not after college or grad school, or even after marriage and fatherhood. Fact of the matter is, I don't know if Holli, or you, or I will ever outgrow the need to be accepted by our peers. We'd all like to be popular. But if the years have taught me anything that I could pass along to Holli and to you, it is this: If fitting in with others means that you must compromise yourself and what you stand for, then "in" ain't really a place you'd want to be.

Replace Myth #23 with this universal truth – *The only way to truly fit in is to create your own mold. Be yourself and 'in' will find you.*

Myth #206 – You don't need to do well in school to be a success in life.

I bet you know a story or two about a dropout who became a millionaire. As a kid I was always ready with a few such examples to share with my folks when they'd go off on one of their *"why aren't your grades better"* routines.

Travis, our 14-year-old resident comic, is also armed with an example that he uses whenever we go off on one of our routines. You see, Trav knows this guy who owns a large construction company, and he never finished high school. Apparently, Travis has interpreted this to mean *"school ain't that important!"*

Don't think for a moment that Travis is dumb. The kid is brilliant; – his grades just don't reflect it. Even though he likely has the highest I.Q. in the house, Travis focuses most of his creative energies on avoiding the educational process. Oh, he likes school – everything but the classroom part.

Travis is not alone. Many teenagers allow the social aspect of school to become more important than the education itself. Their reasoning must be "schoolwork isn't fun, and the rewards aren't immediate, so why bother?"

Travis likes cool stuff, and when he's determined, he usually gets what he wants. What he needs to accept is the fact that his future career, whatever it will entail, will pay him in direct proportion to what he knows. The more he knows, the more he will earn. The more he earns, the more cool stuff he will be able to buy. Armed with the right kind of learned skills, Travis will be in demand; and he may be able to create automation instead of perhaps being replaced by it. Yet this is only one reason he needs a solid education.

If he soaks up the knowledge that his teachers are trying so hard to give him, Travis will be far more effective in solving the challenges that he will face tomorrow. He'll therefore be able to create a better life for himself, and for those who will someday depend on him.

Granted, there are real-life examples of people who've "made it big" without an education. However, if you interviewed them, 99% would claim that their path to success would have been much easier and shorter <u>with</u> an education. And for each such exception you'd uncover, you'd find 5,000 others who had achieved equal or greater success using education as their foundation.

Why gamble against the odds? Take your responsibility as a student very seriously. Because if your teachers appear hard now, the hardest one is still to come. That teacher is experience. It always gives the test first, and the lesson later.

Replace Myth #206 with this absolute truth – *A fish grows to fit the size of its aquarium, and our success is determined by the size of our mental aquarium. Learn and you will earn!*

Myth #783 – Good enough is good enough.

Zac is everything a dad could want in a son, and more. He's a terrific student, a Chicago Bulls/Michael Jordan fanatic, and an avid lover and collector of "Far Side" cartoons. He's truly a blessing from above, but as proud as I am of him, Zac and I are forever locking horns.

To Zac, "good enough" is good enough even when "better" is clearly and easily within his grasp. He compares his efforts and outcomes to those around him, and when he feels his are equal, he stops. Granted, his outcomes generally receive high marks, but Zac has never found out how much Zac can do.

I am forever encouraging Zac to push the envelope. I want him to find all the power that lies inside him. In addition to being a father, speaker, and author, I've also been a teacher, coach, and employer, and I have grown to despise mediocrity.

Never once as a teacher did I give a student an "A" when I knew they were capable of more than they had demonstrated. Never did I put a player in a game who promised to give me a 99% effort. Never did I hire a person who said he'd "try" to show up for work on time or "try" to do a good job. Instead I used the advice of Yoda who said "there is no try – there is only do."

We, as Americans, are so goal-oriented that we forget there is something infinitely more important than reaching our goals; *and that is achieving our potential!*

It would be a crime if the magic inside Zac went unnoticed and untapped. If he is merely content with winning the race against others, he'll stop short of the most important race; the one against himself. I wouldn't want him to go to his grave wishing he had taken advantage of more of the opportunities that were open to him, or that he'd used more of his talents along the way. I'm sure that your parents feel the same way about you.

Why settle for an *average, everyday, ordinary, run-of-the-mill, garden variety* type of existence when you can realize your true potential with just a little more effort? Live life to its fullest by always doing your absolute best in everything you do!

Replace Myth #783 with this paramount truth – *Good enough is never good enough when better is possible!*

Myth #904 – Sticks and stones may break my bones, but names will never hurt me.

Does anyone with a pulse actually believe this ridiculous myth? Certainly not you! After all, you've been the joker – but you've also been the joke**e**. You've been the insult**er** – but you've also been the insult**ee**. And you have been the gossip**er** – but you've also been the gossip**ee**. You've been both an **"er"** and an **"ee"** and you know that it's no fun being an **"ee."**

My daughter Whitney knows. (She's the one who thinks she's eleventeen.) She's an unusually bright, caring, and compassionate girl whose so pretty on the inside you may look past how beautiful she is on the outside. Whitney is only 60 pounds, but 57 of those must be her heart. She is cautious of what she says to others, and she really cares what other people say to her and about her.

Whitney tends to get her feelings hurt a lot. Some of the "richer" girls at her old school made fun of Whitney's clothes because they did not carry a popular brand name. (Keep in mind, these were 9 and 10 year olds!) Recently, she transferred to another school, but she hasn't escaped the cruelty. The boys at this school think it's funny to bark when Whitney walks by, insinuating she is a "dog." I try to convince her that young boys don't know how to approach girls they are attracted to, so they act as if girls are the enemy. But my words are of little comfort. I'd love to tell her that when she gets to high school her classmates will have outgrown this "small-mindedness" – but this is simply not true. Unfortunately, the **"ers"** get meaner as they get older.

On December 4th, I arrived at Fresno's Central High at 8:35 a.m. for an all-school assembly. I wasn't even half way out of my rent-a-car when I heard a teenage girl scream at a group of guys, "Shut up you bunch of $#%^&*!" A teacher quickly grabbed her and asked why she'd unloaded such a verbal barrage. "Everytime I walk by them they 'moo!' I know I'm heavy, but I can't do anything about it!" she cried.

Why do we inflict so much needless pain on each other? Isn't it actually easier to ignore someone than it is to "rip" them? Do we not realize that the cruelty we dish out will eventually come back in our direction?

This much I do know: you can make yours a better school and you can make this a better world if you'll simply choose to stop being an **"er."** Yes, you may still wind up being the **"ee"** every once in a while, but when you consider the fact that it is the **"er"** who is in the most pain, you can rise above it. Heck, you may even decide to show them what kindness feels like.

One day your own child might suffer a wound of the heart, and you, like me, will reflect back to this time in your life and remember how you treated others. You'll want to tell your child that you were kind when you were a kid. You'll want to tell them that the best way to deal with the "ers" is never to become one – no matter what. This way, the "ers" move one step closer to extinction.

Replace Myth #904 with this indisputable truth – *Sticks and stones may break our bones, but names can break our hearts.* Take the high road and be the kind of person you'd want your kids to go to school with.

In conclusion, always remember – Life is full of myths, so you must seek the truth if you want to live the truth. And if a goofy kid named Marty ever asks you to bring a can of yellow spray paint to school, tell him to "bite the wall!"

Not On My Watch

by
BILL CORDES

TEEN
POWER
Too!

Not On My Watch

by
BILL CORDES

I n the movie "A Few Good Men," Tom Cruise plays a young military lawyer defending two Marine privates accused of performing the harsh "Code Red" punishment on Private Willie Santiago. Senior Marines sometimes use this punishment to keep young marines "in line." At one point, one of the privates became upset because he could not understand why he was being punished for performing the "Code Red." He was frustrated and confused because he followed orders and did what he was told. He felt he should not be punished. He said, "I don't understand. What did we do wrong. We did nothing wrong." After a moment of serious thought, the other accused private said, "Yes we did. We were supposed to stand up for people who couldn't fight for themselves. We were supposed to fight for Willie."

The two marines in this movie can teach us a valuable lesson about life and our responsibilities. In the Marine Corps when soldiers are given a post to look after, this post or responsibility is often called their "watch." The first marine felt that if he did exactly as he was told then he was doing his job. The second marine grew to understand that his "watch" was bigger than just doing what he was told. He learned that being a good marine meant not only to do his job but to make decisions while on your "watch" about right and wrong. As a result of reading this chapter, I want the same thing for you. I want you to ask yourself, "What is my watch?" I want you to realize that you have a post to watch after, and the decisions that you make while on your "watch" can build people up or tear them down. You can stand up for what is right on your "watch" and your decisions can make you and others proud.

Choosing to "stand up" is not always easy. Once I chose not to stand up, and there were negative consequences when I did not do "the right thing." There was this kid in my sixth grade class named Albert. He weighed 250 pounds. You can guess what we called him: Fat Albert. I remember when we were introduced. When I heard his name, I immediately laughed, and said, "Fat Albert." He laughed along with me. "That's what they call me." When Albert walked down the hall people chanted, "Hey, Hey, Hey it's FAT ALBERT." Albert was a good sport about his nickname. He would laugh along with us. By looking at him no one ever knew. He reacted as if the kidding and joking did not bother him. In fact, sometimes he even made fun of himself. We would all laugh along with him.

One day we were picking teams at recess. Remember how

you picked teams? "I'll take him. I'll take her," until the last person was left. The last pick was mine. "Oh, man...I'll take Fat Albert." We gave Albert a hard time during the game. We said things like "if we didn't have 'lardo' we might win." Throughout the game we blamed most of our team's failures on Albert. Albert, being Albert, just played along. After recess, we continued to give him a hard time. We ganged up on him and pushed him around. It was fun to push the big kid around. Pushing him around made us feel big and tough. Albert never got angry or upset. He just continued to be Albert: no reaction, no anger. He just played along.

After recess, we came into the classroom. Albert was in his seat with his head down on his desk. I started teasing him again. "Hey, Fat Albert, why is your head down? What's wrong? Come on 'Fatso', look at me." He wouldn't look up. I continued to call him names. I wanted him to look at me. When he finally did, he raised his head and looked straight at me. I saw tears running down both sides of his cheeks. Then I knew. I was responsible for those tears. Have you ever had that feeling? A flush spread across my entire body. I felt the heat of embarrassment. I felt the heat coming up my neck as my face turned red. The disappointment was unbelievable. I was responsible. I was to blame. The good thing was that I learned a lesson. As a sixth grader I learned about feelings and what it means to hurt another person.

I take full responsibility for my actions. I know that what

I did was wrong. There was a lesson to be learned from this experience. I will forever remember the pain that I must have caused Albert. As long as I live I will remember the feeling I experienced as I stood watching Albert cry.

From this experience, I learned that we are raised in a culture that sometimes teaches a lie. Do you remember this rhyme from your childhood?

> Sticks and stones my break my bones
> but words will never hurt me.

I do. This is one of childhood's biggest lies. I knew as a sixth grader it wasn't true, but I acted as if it were true. Even before the incident with Albert, I knew words "hurt." Others' cruel words had hurt me in the past. However, I wanted to fit in with the crowd. I wanted others to like me. I fell into the trap of putting others down to raise myself up. Words hurt!

What I haven't told you about this story is probably the most painful. I share it with you because it teaches a very important lesson. Albert was my friend. Understand me clearly. He wasn't my friend during school. Albert was my friend after school. I couldn't be seen hanging out with Albert during school. What would my friends think? I had a reputation to protect. After all, I was cool. But when the school day ended it was a different story. Albert and I lived close together. I often showed up at his house after school. We had fun and enjoyed hanging out together. During school, however, I would turn into his bully.

Fortunately, Albert was a bigger person than I and I don't mean his size. Despite all the cruel things I said and the horrible way I treated him, Albert remained my friend. And as a friend he taught me a lot. Albert taught me about courage. It takes a lot of courage to go to school in the sixth grade when you weigh 250 pounds! He didn't judge me, even though I was always judging him. He taught me about acceptance. He treated me as he would like to have been treated, even though it must have been difficult for him. Albert had a great sense of humor and that allowed him to laugh at himself. Could we say the same thing in a similar situation? What we didn't realize was that he was laughing on the outside but crying on the inside. That, I think, was an important lesson, too. We are not always what we seem to be.

If you see yourself in my story, you have learned a lesson, too. We all have Alberts in our lives. Who are the Alberts in your life? Who are the people who don't seem to measure up to society's standards? How many times do we pick our friends because they are popular, cool or funny? How often do we make fun of others because they are different, not attractive, or don't seem to measure up? Maybe their supposed shortcomings are not as easy to spot as Albert's. Maybe they have a tougher time with their school work or they have different interests. It is so easy to make others feel bad or seem uncool because they are different.

From time to time everyone feels that we don't measure up. We all face it sometime in our lives. All too often we cope with feeling bad about ourselves by cutting down someone else. It's as if we believe that by pointing out someone else's failures, we become better than that person.

Nothing is further from the truth. Someone once said to me "I can tell how you feel about yourself by the way you treat others." That statement made me think of Albert. Perhaps I did not like myself very much. Our daily actions reflect what's really going on inside of us. These actions can bring us closer to a life of dignity and character if we have the courage to look inside. We must find the courage to do "the right thing" and "stand up."

Albert helped me take the step to look at myself so that I could discover what went on inside. He forced me to realize that we all get to deal with the negative thoughts we have about ourselves. You know those thoughts: "I'm not good enough, I'm not smart enough, I'm too fat, too thin, I'm not coordinated, I'm not as fast or as good as...." It's so easy to get caught into the trap of "I'm not." This makes it hard for us to reach what we are capable of becoming. Throughout our lives we have to come to grips with those situations where we are not as talented, smart, good looking or successful as others. It's easy to look around and see others who are smarter, prettier, better coordinated, more popular, and think, "If only I was like them I would not have any problems." Even the prettiest of the pretty, the smartest of the smart, and the people who seem most talented on the outside have to deal with the negative stuff on the inside.

The true measure of who we are is not found by comparing ourselves to others, but by using the talents and gifts we have. Albert taught me this lesson too. Even though he didn't have all of the apparent "gifts" of the people around him, he worked hard and treated others with respect and dignity. We live in a society that constantly encourages us to compare ourselves to others. We don't realize that these constant comparisons may ultimately leave us with the feeling "I am not good enough." You are good enough and you can start finding that good by reaching out to others.

You can reach out to the Alberts in your life. You can treat them with respect and dignity. Learn from my mistake. I issue this challenge to you because I know something about you. I know that since you had the courage and willpower to pick up this book that you have leadership abilities. Some of your abilities may be untapped, but I know it is there. I also know that you have influence and how you choose to use that influence is what makes the difference. Avoid comparing yourself to others. Instead, focus on how you can improve the gifts and talents you already possess.

This story has been shared with thousands of students in many schools across the United States. Usually, one or two students approach me after an assembly, and say, "Keep telling that story about Albert. I was just like Albert when I was younger." This amazes me because when I look at these students it is hard to imagine why they would not feel good about themselves. When I remember how cruel we can be to each other, then I can understand how anyone, regardless of looks, could feel negatively about themselves.

Think about the Alberts in your life. You know the students at school who may not be as fortunate as you, the ones who struggle in school a little or the ones who are not as popular as others. I want you to think about how you could reach out to them. It could make a difference in their lives. You could read this story and think, "This is a nice story," and go on about your life. I don't think you will. You're too good, too concerned, to settle for something so easy. Go have a real conversation with someone who is outside your peer group. Maybe it's someone who looks as if they don't have many friends. Make a difference in their lives. Don't do it because you feel sorry for them. Do it because the payoff for you will be bigger than you have ever imagined.

The choice we face is simple. Are we going to choose to reach up or to pull down? If we don't feel good about ourselves, we pull others down to our level. If we feel good about who we are, then the sky is the limit. We can choose to make a positive difference in someone's life.

So what can you do to do "the right thing"? First, reach out to others. Realize that everyone has different strengths. Some are bigger, some are stronger, some communicate better, some are more talented, and some are more attractive. It is how we use our strengths to support others that measure our success in life. We can choose to use our strengths and make others feel inferior, but is that why we were given those gifts? What are you doing with your gifts? Find those who need your attention and use your talents and gifts to make a positive contribution in their lives. Second, reach inside to discover more about yourself. In doing so, you will learn and discover leadership qualities you never knew you had. What you do with your life may be an inspiration to others. Third, reach up. Set high goals and expectations for yourself. Don't settle for second best. Be the shining light and voice of hope for your peer group and friends. Make sure that your "watch" is safe and take responsibility for making sure that no one feels inferior around your school while in your presence. Be like the confident Marine sentry and say, **"Not on my watch."** Have your "watch" be a statement of character, respect and dignity. You can see the good in others. You can change their life and yours. You can stand your post and fight for those who need your help. You can and you will "do the right thing."

We All Have Rhythm…And More!

by
DR. LEWIS DODLEY

We All Have Rhythm...And More!

by
DR. LEWIS DODLEY

H ow many of you have ever wanted to know something about a person but were afraid or embarrassed to ask? Unanswered questions can lead to faulty information or naive impressions that are sometimes generated by myths we have about each other and ourselves. In order to deal with talking about myths and things that are not true, it is important to take the position of AMNESTY, which is defined as forgiving and not holding grudges. This type of agreement allows individuals or groups to feel safe in talking and sharing their feelings. I use AMNESTY as an agreement when I am conducting discussions about any of the negative 'isms'. The 'isms' are racism, sexism, adultism, or other negative feelings about a particular group because they are different than you.

MYTHS

Think about it, unfortunately there are many negative myths in our society regarding a lot of groups of people that may be different from me, you, your teacher or others you come in contact with every day. Myths can be defined as a fiction or half-truth, especially one which forms the way people think or feel. Recently I asked a group of local high school students to define myths. They said myths are:

- Tales passed down from people that are exaggerated;
- Folklore, something you can't explain;
- Bits and pieces of truth that are misplaced.

As you can see myths can be passed through families, cultural or ethnic groups or even whole generations. Myths can be told and retold for years, decades, or for as long as anyone can remember. Myths can become so old that nobody remembers anything different and regard the myth as the truth!

The myths we hear about others and ourselves can be buried in our subconscious mind without our awareness that they exist. This will often happen when we've received subliminal messages. Subliminal messages exist or function below our normal level of conscious awareness. In other words, we may believe something but may not fully realize that we believe it. Some of the reasons that subliminal messages work are because they are usually associated with something we like – such as handsome men, pretty women, 'phat' cars, or just having a good time – and the message is constantly repeated. I'll give you a good example of a subliminal message successfully at work. Let's see if I can set this up for you.

SCENE: Marc, a good student in the eleventh grade has just returned home from studying for his finals. He's in the kitchen pouring a large glass of really cold orange juice. From the living room he hears the television and a commercial comes on. Soon Marc hears the words "And … I love you man."

Now what alcohol beverage comes to your mind? That's what I thought of too. Let's test this theory on how subliminal messages work a little further. Would you agree with me that most young people understand right from wrong? Your parents, guardians, teachers, mentors, coaches or allies have all told you about right and wrong for as long as you can remember, right? Well, here is a quick exercise to aid you in understanding first hand how these messages work. Follow these steps and repeat the word below four times, getting louder each time.

1. Ready, say "WHITE" — "WHITE" — "WHITE" — "WHITE!!!"
2. Now answer this question quickly "WHAT DO COWS DRINK?"

How many of you said milk? So did I the first time I tried this exercise. Actually, to be truthful, sometimes when I'm using this exercise I'll think 'milk' too. The reason you think milk and say milk is because you know that cows give milk even though you also know that cows don't drink milk, unless it's a baby calf. But as you've now seen for yourself, if you hear a message long enough, after awhile you will start to believe it yourself. Sometimes without even being aware that you do believe it! So let's start asking questions of ourselves and each other so that myths, especially the negative myths, about people can be ZAPPED out of existence. Let's replace those myths with accurate information about who we really are, and that we really are more alike than different.

Let's now talk about the myths regarding the elders in our society. In our society elders are considered people 50 years old or older. Some people believe the following myths about ALL elders:

MYTHS REGARDING ELDERS:
- Elders cannot drive well or drive too slow;
- Elders can't learn new information. You can't teach an old dog new tricks;
- Elders all play bingo, smell funny, and are always cranky!

The list of elder myths goes on and on. Myths are all around us in our every day life. We hear them about females, males, and teenagers…everyone! Let's explore some of the common myths we've all heard about these groups.

Some people believe the following myths about ALL females:

MYTHS REGARDING FEMALES:
- Females can't drive well or drive all over the road;
- Females can't do math, play sports or read a map;
- Females are just too emotional to be President of the United States!

Are you a female? Do you believe this? Are you a male? Do you believe this? Are you a teenager? Do you believe this? What do you believe? What have you heard about teenagers?

Unfortunately a myth can find it's way into our subconscious and influence our thinking and attitudes about the various groups and cultures that make up America. Let's talk about myths you have probably heard about African Americans. I understand that some of you may be feeling a little nervous about discussing these myths, but I think it's important to address myths in our society that perpetuates stereotypes of people. Have you ever heard myths about ALL African American teenagers?

MYTHS REGARDING AFRICAN-AMERICANS:
- African American teenagers use drugs and are in gangs;
- African American teenagers live in single parent homes on welfare;
- African American teenagers can't be trusted, play basketball every day, and can really dance well.

Do you believe this? Do you believe some of this but not all of it? Are you confused? What do you believe? How many times have you wanted to ask questions about something like racism or sexism but kinda was afraid to ask because you felt you might hurt someone's feelings or they might not understand and hurt your feelings?

FACT: No one is born with a gene to make them any better than anyone else.

I'd like to tell you a personal story; something that happened to me many years ago, but is still applicable today. I hope this will help you to understand what I've been trying to explain. As an African-American college freshman, I remember playing football and I was the only person of color on the whole team. I often felt that I didn't have anyone I could identify with. Often I didn't feel good about myself because of the myths I'd heard about African Americans that influenced me to believe and internalize the idea that my physical traits were negative.

Once after playing in a football game, I hurt my shoulder and instead of getting a cast, my arm was taped to my chest sort of like a sling. That meant the portion of the hair on my chest needed to be shaved so that the tape would attach itself to my skin. The hair on my chest is kinky, just like the hair on my head. When the nurse came into my room to shave my chest I asked her to shave off all of the hair on my chest, not just where the tape was going to be. I wanted her to shave off all the hair on my chest because it was kinky and it didn't look like my the hair on the chests of my teammates. The hair on their chest was straight. I didn't understand why my hair was kinky. Since it was different from everyone else on the team, I felt bad and out of place; like I didn't belong. So ...the nurse went along with my wishes and shaved it all off. At first I felt really proud of my new clean-shaven chest! Now I looked more like my teammates, at least my teammates that didn't have any hair on their chest. But my joy was short-lived. Pretty soon my hair started to grow back. Needless to say, it was very painful, both physically and emotionally when the hair started growing back. I had to look at myself for who I was as a person, what my values and beliefs were. I had to accept myself for who I was kinky hair and all. I was not going to look like my teammates; but then again I looked quite alright anyway! Maybe I could have avoided all that pain if I would have asked questions about my hair and why other people have hair that is different from mine?

What questions do you have?

UNLEARNING

How many of you have questions you would like to ask or know about the opposite sex but are kinda afraid to ask? How many of you have questions you would like to ask or know about a particular race or culture that is different from yours but are kinda afraid to ask?

Often when I am talking with teenagers I commonly encounter questions about Pre-menstrual Syndrome (PMS). These conversations are conducted in 'Safety Circles' where agreements are in place that make the students feel safe to talk (remember AMNESTY agreements discussed earlier in this chapter?). You may be very surprised to know what some young men think PMS is all about. The boys felt safe to discuss their questions about PMS and the girls in the safety circle answered the boys with accurate information about this topic. The accurate information was really a shock to the boys to know that PMS was not what they thought it was. On the other hand one of the questions that stands out for me from the girls is "why are boys so preoccupied with sex." The boys began their response by saying that all boys are not focused on just sex. They continued that the males that are focused just on sex are victims of what they see and hear on television. Often I am told that young people feel that many movie and television roles present stereotypes that makes them feel that being a man means you have to be sexually active, tough, in control, show anger and never cry. These are just a few of the attitudes that are formed because of subliminal messages.

The attitude that a man is "all that" gives a false sense of self. Recently I asked a class of senior high school male students to stand if they had male and female hormones. Guess what happened — no one stood up! Out of 50 boys present, not one boy stood up even though they knew that they had both hormones! I feel this is because they have negative feelings about women based on myths they have probably heard about women. On some level, they felt it was bad to relate to female hormones at all, that to do so would in some way bring question to their manhood.

FACT: We can unlearn the negative things we have heard about each other if:

> We are supplied with accurate information and the experience to talk

> And share with each other.

Let's take the subject of culture, What question do you have about culture but are kinda afraid to ask? I feel that if you know and appreciate the different aspects about another culture you will see some similarities to your own culture. Knowing about a person's **HISTORY** is another aspect that will give you a better picture of how and why a culture responds the way they do, why they may be different from you or different from me. America is referred to as a 'melting pot', but how about calling America a 'tossed salad' because of the different types of cultures in America. Try to find out how and why different cultures came to America, and whether they came here voluntarily or by force. If we all try to understand the different **VALUE AND BELIEF** systems that operate in other cultures it will lead toward a better environment for all people. It is also important to know and accept the various forms of **VERBAL EXPRESSION** that different cultures use. I think that would certainly aid in better communication among all of us.

There is an exercise I often use in adult groups and teen groups called *Cultural Assessment.* The participants are asked to identify the various aspects such as those underlined above and indicate whether the aspect is a myth or is part of a culture. First they try it based on their own culture, then based on any other culture that they are less knowledgeable about. This exercise not only helps to understand how myths influence our thinking, but also shows how we are more alike than different. How would you

feel if you were taught to believe that a man is never supposed to cry or women are not pretty unless they are very
thin? These attitudes can wreck havoc on anyone's self-
esteem. So we have to unlearn the negative stuff.

SOLUTIONS

The Seven Principles of the Nguzo Saba are African principles of life that are as old as mankind and applies to us
all regardless of our cultural origin. These seven principles apply to all of our lives and are principles we can
live by.

The Seven Principles of the Nguzo Saba are as follows:

1. **UNITY** helps us to come together against the 'isms',
    racism; sexism; adultism and accept people for who
    they are.

2. **SELF-DETERMINATION** helps us learn our cul-
    tural history so that we can define ourselves and others
    will not define who we are and how we see ourselves.

3. **COLLECTIVE WORK AND RESPONSIBILITY**
    means helping to support community projects such
    as planting trees or recycling regardless of race, gen-
    der or age.

4. **COLLECTIVE ECONOMICS** is working for com-
    mon economic goals such as pulling together to hold
    a bake sale or wash cars to raise money for a class trip.

5. **PURPOSE** can be found in activities such as developing 'Safety Circles' in schools or community organizations to teach each other about cultural issues.

6. **CREATIVITY** means using creative ways to deal with problems instead of using the 'flight or fight' syndrome to confront conflict.

7. **FAITH** means having faith in ourselves and the belief that the human spirit is able to adopt positive attitudes about each other when we unlearn the negative myths we have been taught.

So, my dear friends, good luck to you all! Forget the myths and remember the facts!

FACT: We all got rhythm!

Sex, Drugs, 'N' Rock 'N' Roll

by
JULIE EVANS

Sex, Drugs, 'N' Rock 'N' Roll

by
JULIE EVANS

So, you wanna' have a party?

Who will you invite?

Did you know that almost 2 billion teenagers live on planet Earth? Now that's a party!

While your parents and teachers don't want to think about 2 billion teens having a party, I say party on! Young people worldwide have done incredible things by hanging out and having a good time.

Last year in the United States, teens volunteered about 1.6 billion hours of volunteer time. If we had hired you it would have been equivalent to hiring 966,800 full time employees which would cost about 7 billion dollars!

You are amazing.

Yet so many young people get a bad rep. Why?

Is it from "old" people and newspapers generating ugly statistics about teen pregnancy, violence, gangs, drop outs and AIDS?

Maybe it's the music you listen to, your clothes or the friends you hang out with. I mean, how many of you have ever been blamed for something you didn't do? Or, received a grade you didn't deserve? Or, not been appreciated for something?

I guess it depends on what story you read. I know for a fact that many young people change laws, save animals, feed the homeless, spend time with elderly, raise money for hospitals, build teen centers, protect forests, work with younger students and get involved. These teens know what it takes to be a leader of their own life and in turn make life happen for themselves and the world around them.

What's your story?

While I was in Alaska speaking to teens about being leaders of their own lives, three boys dared each other to shoot another boy just for the fun of it. The boy died and the three pranksters went to jail. Why? Because they turned their lives over to somebody else. They let somebody else influence their decisions.

Reverend Jim Jones convinced over 900 members of his

San Francisco based People's Temple to go with him into the jungles of Guyana and commit group suicide by drinking cyanide. Under his guidance, mothers were told to force their small children to drink the cyanide before killing themselves. Why? Because they turned their lives over to someone else. They lived somebody else's story.

SEX, DRUGS, 'N' ROCK 'N' ROLL is about being a leader of your own life. It's about knowing your own story. Understanding who you are and making decisions about your own life based on the outcomes you want for yourself, your friends, your family and your community.

And, that takes courage.

Cult groups and gangs provide extreme examples of how some people choose to live somebody else's story. Yet, to much lesser degrees all of us face pressures that challenge who we are. Perhaps your friends want you to act a certain way that doesn't feel right. Or maybe, you try to act like an older brother, sister, or adult in ways that don't fit your personality.

It takes courage to become a LEADER of your own life. Especially when you feel down and out and lonely.

Have you ever felt lonely?

When I was 12 my mother attempted suicide. She lived in a mental hospital for three months and then six months later…I was 13 at the time…my mother abandoned my family. I haven't heard from her since. Talk about feeling alone.

Who me? Julie? Alone? I was the first girl student body president of my elementary school. In 7th grade I served on student council and even though I lost by 3 votes for vice president of the school in 8th grade, I was a popular kid. People liked me. And, then my mother jumped ship and my world turned upside down.

I felt so alone.

I remember sitting on my window sill with my stuffed animals from my childhood around me. As I gazed out the window at the trees below, I clasped my hands, closed my eyes and started to pray.

"Dear God, if I keep my eyes closed for 30 seconds exactly…will you let my Mom walk out from behind that tree?"

My mom never did come out from behind the tree. I felt so alone.

My world started to fall apart. I couldn't think. I started to isolate myself from other people. Everyone seemed different from me. And, I started to do things I'm not proud of. I got into trouble, sex and too many chocolate chip cookies. And, before I knew it, my grades dropped and I gained twenty pounds. I was no longer a leader of my own life. I turned into a victim of other people.

What I learned, I learned the hard way. If I could go back in time I'd realize that I wasn't alone. Everybody has a story. Some people live with parents who drink too much, argue too much, or don't have enough money. Some of us experience divorce, sick relatives or pesty siblings. And, even if that's not your story, everybody has bad days.

It's not what happens to you, but what you do with it that makes a difference. And, that takes courage. It takes courage to become a LEADER of your own life.

The "L" for being a LEADER of your own life stands for LIKING YOURSELF. Whether you have a good hair day, a bad hair day or a no hair day; it means you can look in the mirror and say "I like myself" no matter what anyone else says or does to you. This can seem especially hard when people put you down, especially your friends. Sometimes, grownups think they can motivate you by making you feel bad.

"Young man, get those hands out of your pockets!"

"Young lady, you go out looking like that, you know what they'll say about you!"

"If you had brains for ink, you wouldn't have enough ink to dot an i !"

You know what I'm talking about. You have to like yourself no matter what.

The "E" for being a LEADER of your own life stands for EMPATHY, compassion for other human beings.

Have you ever been left out? Overlooked for a spot on the team? The part in the play? Not invited to the party?

Most of us have felt left out at some time.

Unfortunately, life isn't fair.

We live in a world that has racism, sexism, ageism, handicapism and big-noseism. People who think like that are <u>not</u> leaders of their own lives.

I'll never forget the day Bill invited me to eat lunch with him. He was definitely the finest boy in school and hung out with the most popular group. On my way to eat lunch with Bill, Julia approached me and asked me what I was doing coming over to their tree. When I explained that Bill had invited me for lunch, Julia replied, "You're not welcome here. We don't like you!"

"Why?"

"Because you smile too much!"

Julia had no idea how much I needed a friend, or how much pain I was feeling about losing my Mom. She missed an opportunity to be a leader. Being a leader is not about being popular, it's about thinking for yourself. We must offer compassion and treat each other with respect, especially if it's not popular.

The "A" in being a LEADER of your own life stands for ATTITUDE - a positive attitude.

Each of us creates thousands of thoughts everyday. To the degree these thought are positive we feel better about ourselves, achieve our goals and people want to eat lunch with us. To the degree in which these thoughts are negative we sabotage our life. Since most people only think one thought at time, it makes sense to focus on the positive.

Our minds solve problems based on what we think about. If we think we'll never make new friends, we probably won't. However, if we believe we can make new friends, our minds will look for opportunities to make and improve friendships.

The more often we think about something, the more our brain registers the image as important. One way to help you focus on the positive is to identify what strengths you already have. For example, if you think you'll never do well in math, it will make studying harder. However, if you can recall what strengths helped you do better in another challenging situation (let's say a sports event) you can apply the same principles towards doing better at mathematics.

My friend Louise is an accomplished skier who decided to take up snowboarding. After flailing a few times on the slopes she thought she'd never make it as a snowboarder. Her friends reminded her how often she fell while learning to ski. Louise remembered how her sense of humor about falling made learning to ski fun. Once Louise applied her sense of humor to boarding, she was able to focus on the positive. This made snowboarding less difficult.

Most of us feel surprised by how many strengths we have. Strengths come in many shapes and sizes. There are inner qualities such as being honest, caring, drug-free, non-violent, determined and friendly. These are qualities nobody can take away from you. You also have specific abilities: sports, school subjects, creative talents and leadership. Sometimes our strengths come from the outside world including one's family, friends and where we live.

Your strengths and your attitude impact who you are in the world. When you feel good about yourself you elicit feelings of well-being from those around you. You become more attractive to others.

What's your attitude? What strengths do you have? How can you use your strengths to pull yourself up when you're feeling down?

The "D" in being a leader of your own life stands for DO-ING SOMETHING THAT MAKES A DIFFERENCE.

Help yourself…your friends…your family…. Help your community.

Now is the time to make life happen. The difference between dreaming and doing has to do with taking action. Decide what your passion is and go for it.

When Gennie Sluder and her high school friends learned how 1-out-of-3 Oregon children go to school hungry they decided to coordinate a state-wide program on local hunger. Gennie and her friends challenged Oregon high schools and local businesses to donate food and money to help local students. They made a difference to the tune of 12,000 cans of food and $6,000 for local food banks.

Where do you need to make a difference in your life and the lives of others?

The second "E" is for ENTHUSIASM. If you're going to DO SOMETHING - DO IT with ENTHUSIASM.

And, while nothing great was ever accomplished without enthusiasm, it is often that rush of excitement that pushes us to act without thinking.

Have you ever done something with so much enthusiasm that you said or did something that got you in trouble?

That's why the "R" in being a LEADER of your own life stands for RESPONSIBILITY.

You don't live in a "just say no" or "just say yes" world. You live in a world where people have choice. Yet, many of us have the "Just Do It" attitude and forget to think about what we're doing. Freedom comes from making choices that have a positive effect on yourself, your friends, your family and your community.

Too often we get stuck on that island called "Someday I'll." You know that island....

Someday I'll finish my homework ahead of time...

Someday I'll help Mom or Dad with the chores before they ask...

Someday I'll ask that boy or girl out...
learn snowboarding... take karate... dance...
paint... play guitar... start a rock band....

Sometimes we get stuck on that island called "Someday I'll" because we don't know how to do something, or we're hanging out with the wrong friends, or we're just plain lazy. Yet, if we took the time to think about our choices we'd gain the power and control we're looking for.

Dr. Dureyea at the University of New Mexico studied young people much like you. He found that teenagers who took at least 4 -10 seconds to make a decision made better choices than if they didn't take that time to think. Choices like getting in a car with an intoxicated driver, yet drinking and driving is one of the four top causes of death for people your age.

Four Top Causes of Death
- Drinking & Driving
- Suicide
- Homicide
- AIDS

FOUR seconds can be the difference between life or death. FOUR seconds can be the difference between friendship and heartache. FOUR seconds can be the difference between having what you want and not having it.

Powerful choices require powerful thinking. Use your own insight by taking at least 4 seconds to think about what you want for yourself, your friends, your family and your community.

L: LIKE YOURSELF
    No matter what other people say or do to you.
E: EMPATHY
    Compassion for others even if it's not popular.
A: ATTITUDE
    A Positive Attitude.
D: DO SOMETHING TO MAKE A DIFFERENCE
    For yourself & others.
E: ENTHUSIASM
    Yes, I can.
R: RESPONSIBILITY
    To take at least 4 seconds to become...

A LEADER OF YOUR OWN LIFE.

And, that takes courage… To like yourself… Stand up for what you believe… Think for yourself… Risk something new… And, show the world you can do it!

Students ask me, "What about you, Julie? Was it hard for you to become a leader of your own life? I mean, you lost your mom at thirteen…."

And, I answer — "YES! LIFE ISN'T FAIR."
"NO ONE SAID LIFE IS EASY."
"FIND YOUR OWN DREAM AND MAKE IT COME TRUE."

BEING A LEADER OF YOUR OWN LIFE is only for the courageous and the brave.

Today, I speak to over 100,000 students each year and I've addressed audiences in 33 states, 4 islands and Canada. I speak about being a leader of your own life. Maybe you'll decide to lead others and help make our world a more peaceful place for everybody.

With 2 billion teens on this planet, you can make a world of difference. What kind of party do you want? Who do you want to invite? How about inviting everybody?

Imagine what would happen if 2 billion teens came together for world peace? To end world hunger? Came together for a heathy planet? Imagine….

What can happen if you take 4 seconds to think about what you want for yourself... your friends... your family... For your community....

Imagine yourself being a leader of your own life.

You are amazing. There is only one you. You pass this way just once.

You have the courage!

Go out and DO IT!

The Seed

by
ED GERETY

The Seed

by

<u>ED GERETY</u>

"**I** can't make it," she cried, "My arms are tired and my knee hurts. Please pull me up!!!!!" These were the words that echoed off the Otter Cliffs in Acadia National Park from Alexis, a sixteen year old, during her first rock climbing experience. It was towards the end of the day and the six other students on the trip had all repelled the 90 foot cliff. The cliff went straight down onto a charcoal black rock ledge which then descended into the Atlantic Ocean. All of the students had successfully rock climbed back up and Alexis was the last to go. She was a strong-minded, sensitive kid who had lately found herself getting into trouble at school and at home. There had been no specific reason for this recent behavior except that she was feeling stressed out and overwhelmed with everything. She had come on this trip because a friend of hers had said that it would be a good time and that it might help her to figure some things out.

Each time she thought her hand or foot had found a new crevice or a new spot to move her upwards, she would slip and fall only to have the climbing harness catch her. Alexis was hot and tired. The chalk from her hands was beginning to get in her eyes. With rage in her voice she yelled," Pull me up! I quit, I hate this. This is stupid!"

It was at that moment when Jason, the head counselor on the trip, looked at me and said, "Ed, I'm going to go down and talk with her."

I then yelled down to Alexis, "Hold on! You can do this. We know you can!"

Jason grabbed another rope, put his climbing harness on and began to repel down the cliff. Within moments Jason was beside Alexis. She had her cheek directly against the face of the rock with her feet barely resting on a small piece of the cliff that jetted outward. Jason said to Alexis, "I know that you have been on this cliff now for what seems like a very long time. Your feet and fingers are cramping up and your forearms feel as though they are on fire. But, Alexis, you are strong, look how far up you are already. You have taken one of the more difficult paths up the cliff. Look Alexis, look at the path you have taken."

At that moment, Alexis moved her cheek away from the rock face and looked down. The bright white chalk she used on her hands to give her a better grip, showed the trail where her tired hands had moved her upward on the cliff. Jason was right, Alexis had taken the hardest way up the cliff. Jason then looked straight into Alexis' eyes and in a calm voice he said, "You are not alone out here, there are people who care about you, who want to help you and see you succeed. We are going to do this together. Are you ready?" Hesitantly she shook her head yes and took a deep breath.

The secret to getting up the cliff is to take it one step at a time. Sometimes we are in such a rush to get to the top that we miss a spot that will help us move a step closer to our goal. It's okay to fall and slip, even to rest, as long you begin climbing again no matter how many times you fall.

"Alexis, I know that you can do this, you know that you can do this." Words of encouragement began to echo down from the students up above as Alexis began to slowly crawl upwards. Jason was right beside her as she made each move. He was not telling her where to go or what to do. Instead, he was reminding her of the power that she had within her to get to the top. You see, sometimes we forget that we already have the power and the resources to help us reach our goals. At any moment in our lives we can tap into that power and reach a new level. Only if we are willing to take the risk to let go of what is familiar and secure in our lives, and reach out to something that is new and different.

"Almost there, hold on, hang in there, you can do it, don't give up!!" Finally, with one last pull by her tired hands, Alexis found herself on top of the cliff. She was greeted by high-fives, slaps on the back, and wide-eyed smiles.

Looking back on her first experience at rock climbing, Alexis said that the event reminded her of where she was right now in her life, somewhat unsure of where to go next. She needed to remind herself to continue to move forward and that she was not alone in dealing with the pressures that she was going through. Alexis is like most kids her age. She is trying to do well in school and find a group of friends that will bring out the best in her. A group of friends that will accept her for the person that she is. She hopes to make the varsity softball team and be accepted into a good college. Out there on the cliff, Alexis was reminded that there were people there to help her. Rock climbing is very much like life, because each person chooses her own path and like life, that is what makes it so special and such a challenge. The lessons that we learn in life are taught to us in so many different ways. They could be through the adventure of rock climbing, an unexpected experience with a close friend, being part of a team, or even right in a classroom.

For example, not too long ago I was visiting a small first grade classroom in Hampton Falls, New Hampshire. The first thing I noticed when I walked in were the tiny seats. They sat low under neatly arranged desks. The entire classroom was covered in colorful art. Each picture had the student's name written on it in bold letters which showed how proud they were of their work. The teacher said, "Class, please put down your pencils and say hello to our special guest, Mr. Gerety."

All of a sudden, eighteen of the cutest little kids you have ever seen said in unison, "HELLOOOOO Mr. Gerety."

I asked, "How are you today, class?" They all responded, "Gooooood!!!"

The teacher then said to me, "Mr. Gerety, come over here and sit down."

I then heard a couple of the kids whisper, "Cool, he gets to sit in the special chair."

I was guided to the corner of the classroom, which was the reading center, and I sat down into an old wooden rocking chair. It was surrounded by a four inch thick, green, red and purple carpet which had a peculiar smell. The eighteen first graders all sat Indian-style around me and I asked, "Does any one have any questions?"

Boom !!! Almost all the hands shot up into the air with sounds of "oh, oh, I do, I do!" Quickly, I called on one student. I asked what her name was and after a long pause she said, "Suzie," somewhat unsure of her answer.

I asked, "What is your question Suzie?"

"Is it true, how come, ummm, oops I forgot."

"That's okay, I'll come back to you later." I asked another, "What is your name?"

He answered, "Chip."

"What is your question Chip?" He said, "Mr. Gerety, do you want to see what it is we are doing?"

I said, "Sure Chip." The next thing I know, Chip stood up and walked to the windowsill of the classroom. I got up and followed Chip. Seventeen other kids got up and followed me. Chip reached to the windowsill and pulled down a milk carton which was cut in half. He held it the way you and I would hold a newborn baby. Carefully, he moved closer to me and said with excitement in his voice, "Look Mr. Gerety, look what we're doing."

The milk carton was filled half way with dirt, and a little green thing was coming out of the center. Now, being the excited person that I am, I said, "Wow what are you doing in there, growing a pine tree?"

Chip just shook his head and replied, "No Mr. Gerety, we are growing a flower."

"Tell me Chip, how did you grow that flower?" He said, "First thing we had to do, Mr. Gerety, is get some good dirt, not bad dirt, but good dirt."

I said, "OK Chip, then what happened?"

"Well, everyone in the class was given one seed and the teacher said we better not eat it, because we were not getting another. We then had to plant the seed one finger nail length beneath the soil. But see Mr. Gerety," as he put his finger 1/2 inch from my nose, "I had to go a whole knuckles length because my finger is so small."

I said, "I can see Chip. Then what happened?"

"Then we had to give it a little bit of water, a little bit of sun, but not too much."

"When do you check on it?"

"Before snack and after recess."

I held up the milk carton to look for Chip's name on the bottom of it, but his name was not on it. In fact, there was no name on it at all, so I looked at Chip and asked, "Chip, is this flower yours?"

He said, "yes," then he said, "well no."

I asked, "Well which one is it?"

He said, "I'm not sure."

"YOU'RE NOT SURE?" I said, loudly. "You mean to tell me, Chip, that the seventeen other milk cartons all along that window sill, not one of them has a name on it?"

He said, "No, Mr. Gerety."

I asked, "Then tell me Chip, how do you know which one is whose?" Chip looked up at me, kind of surprised that I did not know the answer and said, "Well, we don't, Mr. Gerety. We just take care of every one." Then the little boy next to him responded enthusiastically, "Then we get to take them home."

The important lessons that were being taught to those first graders are as important today as they were in the first grade. They are the importance of working together, supporting one another, and believing in something even if at first you cannot see it.

Through school and throughout your entire life there will be wonderful, joyful moments when you feel as though everything is perfect. There will also be times in your life when you are going to be faced with set backs, disappointments, and things that don't turn out the way you expect them to. It is during these times when you need to remember that you have the power to believe in yourself and to make the choice to not give up, and that you are not alone. There are people who care about you, who want to help you, and who love you very much.

There is a scene in the movie, <u>The Lion King</u>, when Mufasa is walking with his son Simba, and Mufasa explains to him that, "We must all take our place in the circle of life.... For each one of us has a place which is ours and ours alone."

Never forget that you play a unique and special part in

the circle of life. Without you in it, the circle of life would not be complete. You have gifts and talents that make the circle of life the special circle that it is. So continue to explore, dream, and discover all that lies ahead of you in this great journey of life.

Who Packs The Parachute?

by
PATRICK T. GRADY

Who Packs The Parachute?

by
PATRICK T. GRADY

Change...a six letter word that puts fear in the hearts of millions of individuals throughout the entire world. Why? Because too often we worry about the negative aspects of a change instead of the positive ways in which it can be of benefit to all of us. As leaders we must be open to the ideas of others, we must listen to the thoughts of those we are leading and we must weigh the benefits that change can offer.

All of us, no matter how young or old, go through tremendous changes in our lives on a daily basis.

One of the greatest things that ever happened in my life was the fact that I found someone willing to marry me. My wife is 5' 9" tall and I am only 5' 7". This difference in height has been the subject of numerous jokes from family and friends. But I always tell her, "Honey, it's better to have loved a short man than to never have loved a-tall."

For our first anniversary I decided I wanted to do something different. Having addressed hundreds of groups and discussed the importance of trying things that are new and of being open to positive change, I decided to practice what I preach.

A gift for my new bride had to be something original. Flowers were too common, jewelry would be expected, and I didn't want to take her to some fancy restaurant like...the Waffle House. For weeks I pondered over what to get my new bride. Finally, one evening while watching a movie on television, it hit me.

We were watching a movie called "Point Break" starring Patrick Swayze. During this picture they go sky diving. My wife said, "You know, I've always wanted to go sky diving."

My wife is a very adventuresome individual. She has been whitewater rafting, parasailing, snorkeling in the Bahamas, and rode a mule to the bottom of the Grand Canyon. Therefore, I decided I'd surprise her. We live in Charlotte, North Carolina, and the following Monday morning I phoned a company in Chester, South Carolina, called Skydive Carolina. I made an appointment to go sky diving the Saturday morning following our first anniversary. I told my wife nothing about it (this was to be totally unexpected). I informed her that we were going to a local park for a picnic with friends. On Saturday morning the alarm clock went off, I got dressed, and hurried downstairs to wait for my new bride. Eventually she came down the stairs, looking quite lovely in a sundress.

The thought of my new bride, free-falling from an airplane with her sundress billowed around her head, didn't seem appropriate. So, I convinced her to change and we left for the "park." We traveled down Interstate 77 to Chester, South Carolina, and turned off the "hard road" onto an unpaved, unmowed "pig-trail." There at the end was the airport. My wife saw the Skydive Carolina sign and was enthusiastic about the activities yet to come.

The airport consisted of a double-wide mobile home. This was the air traffic control tower, training facility, snack bar, and tanning salon. When we registered inside, the receptionist informed us that our training would begin as soon as the pilot finished mowing the runway. I began to wonder if we would live to see our second anniversary.

Eventually our instructor came in and introduced himself. We were then escorted, along with numerous other "first-timers," to a back room for instruction. We viewed several videos that discussed the intricate details of sky diving, we were introduced to the equipment, given a description of what to expect, and asked if we had any questions.

My question, of course, was, "Who packs the parachute?" His reply, "You do."

Having never packed a parachute in my life, I realized that the instructor knew the secret to my success, so therefore I followed every direction exactly as it was given.

We, along with other first-timers and professionals, boarded our aircraft...a 1942 Beechcraft. I wasn't even born until 1962, so you can imagine my concern. The plane leapt down that grassy runway and took off. We climbed to our maximum cruising altitude of 10,500 feet.

The professionals exited the plane and created fancy formations by grabbing ankles and elbows. Now it was time for the first timers to exit! I have never been so embarrassed in my life. Imagine a grown man, standing at the door of that aircraft, whimpering, crying, whining, and acting like such a weanie!!!

They got **ME** quiet...and we exited the plane. Here I was, free-falling from 10,500 feet at approximately 120 miles per hour and, thanks to my mother, the only thing I could think was..."In case I have an accident, I hope I have on clean underwear!"

Eventually, I pulled the rip cord and the parachute opened perfectly.

I began to wonder how many people follow the same ruts and routines day in and day out. How many of us fail to create our future and merely stand by and watch things happen?

I'm not saying that we must all go bungy-cord jumping or *heaven forbid* jump out of a perfectly good airplane. What I am saying is that we are responsible for our futures. We are responsible for ourselves and where we will end up on the road of life. *Our minds are like parachutes...they only work when they're open.* **You and I are responsible for packing our own parachutes for our free-fall into life.**

This means that we must open our minds to a tremendous future, for the decisions we make today will directly impact our lives tomorrow.

Everyone makes choices and decisions on an hourly basis. We make some decisions that to many may seem minor. For example: What time we will arise in the morning? What we will eat for breakfast? What we will wear to school or work? During the same day we may have to make major decisions, such as: Will I study for final exams? Should I apply for scholarships? What is the best way to lead those who elected me?

When the time comes to make both minor and major decisions, try asking yourself some of the following questions:

- Is this the right thing to do? Yes or No? If the answer is yes, do it. If the answer is no, find the right thing to do.
- Does this choice support my values and beliefs?
- Does this decision show my true character?

- Will I be proud of this decision?
- Whom, besides me, will this decision affect?
- What are the possible outcomes of this choice?
- Will the choice I am about to make benefit me, my family, or the ones I am leading?

Another tool you may use in making correct choices is:

- Whom do I admire the most?
- Why do I admire this person?
- Do I admire his/her character, values, and beliefs?
- What would he/she do in this situation?
- Call that person, ask questions, and for advice.
- Listen to the thoughts of parents, teachers, clergy, friends, etc.
- Weigh the information you receive and make an educated decision.

Try to imagine situations ahead of time and think about how you would respond. Ask the question, "What if...." For example: "What if peers were encouraging me to make a destructive choice (alcohol/drinking and driving/drugs/sex/breaking curfew/not studying, etc.). What would I do? How would I handle this situation? What options do I have?" This can be an effective tool in preparing ourselves for the unexpected.

Every decision we make during our lives is not perfect,

and occasionally we will make wrong choices, that's part of life. **But if we learn from our mistakes, then they become lessons!**

Our next step is to stand up for what we believe in and to take responsibility for our actions. We seem to live in a day and age in which people around the world do not take responsibility for themselves. We want to blame someone else for our problems.

After delivering a keynote address to a group of middle school students, I was visiting with a fifth grader who informed me that he was in trouble at home. I inquired as to what happened. He replied, "I forgot to feed the dog." "Is that your job," I asked. "Yes, sir, I'm supposed to feed the dog everyday." "Well," I said, "Why didn't you feed the dog?" He said, "After school the other day, my friends came over to my house to play football and we had a great time. We played until dark and I went in the house to eat dinner. My dad asked me if I'd fed the dog and I told him I hadn't. He got mad and put me on restriction." I said, "Whose fault was it?" He said, "The dog's!"

I told him, "It's not the dog's fault, it's yours! You had a job to do and you didn't do it; therefore, you must face the consequences, which in this case is restriction."

Everyone has a job to do. That job is to prepare ourselves in the best way possible for the future. We do not know what the future holds, but we do hold our future. We are responsible for ourselves. Where we end up tomorrow or twenty years from now depends on the choices we make today. We must continue to educate our minds and work as hard as possible to lay a solid foundation upon which we can build.

No one in this world owes you or me anything! If we want the best out of life, we must earn it. Life is not easy, it takes hard work, education, good decision making skills, and the support and encouragement of one another.

As leaders and citizens of the United States, we must respect one another for who we are. Let's take time to get to know our neighbors. If we are in a position of leading others, it is imperative that we listen to their thoughts, find out their likes and dislikes, opinions, and beliefs. There are hearts beating around us each and every day. True, some hearts are beating to a different drummer; however, it's the "different" beats/tunes/tones that make beautiful music.

During leadership conferences and summer camps, directed by my friend Randy Kilby, we divide delegates into groups of approximately ten members each and have them participate in an activity we call "Insights." During this program the groups go through a series of questions that allow them, in a very short period of time, to find out a great deal about each other. Every person is required to answer all questions. The questions range from your favorite color to the qualities you look for in a close personal friend.

Participating in one particular conference was a young lady named Maria. Maria was a great deal like any other student leader attending the program, with the exception of one physical difference. That difference was that she was missing the middle finger on each hand. Because of this handicap, she was treated as an outsider by most of the participants. Instead of others initiating conversation with Maria, they seemed to exclude her from the group. Many of those attending centered their conversations around her hands. One could overhear people saying, "Did you see her hands? That looks awful! I wonder what happened."

During "Insights" one of the questions posed is, "What do you hate the most?" Of course a wide variety of answers were given, "I hate my little brother, he's such a pain," "I hate homework and studying for tests," "I hate getting up so early in the morning for school or work." When it was Maria's time to answer, tears were streaming down her face and she said, "I hate my father!" She went on to explain why and added, "When I was a little girl, my father got mad at me and he cut my fingers off."

Dead silence! It seemed as if no one could take a breath.

What happened next was truly amazing. Suddenly, a feeling of compassion overcame the group. Now, instead of Maria being an outsider with hands that were different from everyone else's, she became a person, and the delegates offered her their hands, hearts, hugs, and love.

Why? Because now we knew the rest of the story.

What Maria had gone through with her father was a terrible ordeal. Now she had to deal with the constant rejection and ridicule of others for the rest of her life. Why? Because she was different in *appearance*. Maria was judged not by what was inside but by what showed on the outside.

We have more in common with one another than we might think. Many times we base our opinions of others on the way they look as opposed to the way they think.

Everyone on the face of this Earth is different, and that is wonderful. If we all walked the same, talked the same, thought the same, looked the same, and acted the same, what a boring place this would be! Instead of concentrating on the negative differences between us, let's look for the positive attributes of others, because, I'll promise you, **much greater are the things that unite us than the things that divide us.**

After delivering a keynote address to a group of educators attending a conference, I had the opportunity of visiting with one of the delegates, a kindergarten teacher. As most speakers will agree, one of the highlights of any program is the time spent with the people present and discovering the positive differences they are making in the lives of others.

Now just about everyone, no matter how old he or she is,

can remember his or her kindergarten or first grade teacher. These individuals have a special rapport with their students and an everlasting impact upon their lives.

Mrs. Johnson, had been working with children for many years and loved her work immensely, and she told me the following story:

About half way through the school year, tragedy struck my family. Very unexpectedly my mother passed away, and I immediately left school to make final arrangements for her burial and to settle family matters. I cannot begin to describe the pain and anguish I felt from losing my mother and the depression that followed.

It seemed that not only had I lost my mother but also a large part of myself. I went through a wide range of emotions from pain, anger, and finally self pity. Two weeks later I returned to the classroom and to my students but did not realize that I had not fully recovered from the shock and grief of losing my mother. Nor did I understand how much I had changed in such a short period of time.

At the end of my first week back in the classroom one little girl asked me, "Mrs. Johnson, what's wrong?" I replied, "What do you mean?" She said, "You aren't like you were before you went on vacation."

"Well," I said, "You know how you love your mommy?" The little girl replied, "I love my mommy very much." I said, "My mommy just died and I have been very sad."

The young girl replied, "Did your mommy live until she died?"

I smiled and said, "Why, of course she did, honey."

With that the child said, "Mrs. Johnson, you need to live until you die!"

Let's live until we die. Choose to live life to its fullest. Be optimistic. Look for the best in yourself and others. Educate your mind. Treasure your family and friends.

This chapter is dedicated to the memory of:

Randy Keith Kilby
(1955-1997)
My hero. My friend.

All's Fair...

Except Maybe Your Parents!

by
MICAH JACOBSON

All's Fair...
Except Maybe Your Parents!
by
MICAH JACOBSON

D o you look at the world sometimes and think, "Hey, that's not fair!" Maybe you've said, "I ought to drive that Ferrari, not some guy with fifteen gold chains dangling on his hairy chest, which you can clearly see since his shirt is unbuttoned to his navel." Or, "I should have gotten an A on that math test, not the girl who sits next to me and thinks cans of hair spray have to be used all at once."

Thoughts of inequality plague most of us. You may not feel this way, because I've heard you're perfect, but I get jealous occasionally when someone has something that I want. Kind of like women who wish they could spit more often. OK, maybe that's a bad example.... Although I must admit that spitting is really fun sometimes. But then again, I don't get out much.

I used to complain to my dad that life wasn't fair. Where do dads learn "dad lines"? Do they go to parental comeback school? My dad had some beauts. I'd say, "I'm hungry." He'd answer with the witty comeback, "Hi, hungry, I'm your father!" Very funny. I'd say, "Hey that's not fair," as my brother got to practice using the VCR remote control while I had to wax the kitchen floor with my mom's mascara brush. (I'm kidding, of course.... Usually, Mom would never let me touch her mascara brush.... I guess I'm happy about that now.) Dad would turn around and say, "Oh, you want fair? Why don't you do my job for awhile and I'll go to school. That's fair, right?" (Why are parents compelled to say dumb things? It must be genetic.... Oops, I hope not!) Every once in a while my dad would actually come up with something fairly intelligent, like, "Fair?! Who ever promised fair? Now get to work!" That response sounded reasonable. No one *had* ever promised fair. But every kid I know has uttered those infamous words at some point. Something inside us yearns for life to be fair.

I think women learn that life is unfair before men do. It's not that men ignore life's inconsistencies (OK, maybe some do), but women certainly seemed forced to confront these issues face-to-face: "How come he gets to go to the bathroom standing up and I...." Well, you get the idea. My girlfriends (oops, I mean my female friends. Hey, how come girls can call their female friends girlfriends, but guys can't call their male friends boyfriends? That's not fair. Can you imagine, "Sorry, honey, I can't go out with you tonight because I am going out with my boyfriends"? Hmmm, it doesn't seem to have the same ring, does it? But back to my point.) seem to have learned about life's inequalities before any of the men I know. Which reminds me, how come women always get to go first? I mean, this whole women-and-children-first rule must have been made up by women and children, which is not to say that I reject the idea of chivalry. If I were on a sinking ship, I would certainly offer my seat on the lifeboat to the nearest woman or child (unless they moved too slow... I'm kidding, I'm kidding). But I want to be able to choose – I want to know I could have taken the seat, but that I made a heartfelt decision that this newborn child (wearing a precious pink bonnet, and with her whole life as a world-class neurosurgeon ahead or her) ought to have it. I think you see where I'm coming from, unless you're a woman, and then you might be saying, "Oh, puhleeese. Men have nothing to complain about. They have life so good, and they don't even realize it." You know what? We men, for the most part, don't know how good we have it ...which is precisely my point. Life is not fair.

So the question becomes, why fight it? I think, in some ways, that we have to fight it. We must continue to struggle for fairness, justice, love, and compassion. Sometimes it's hard to come by these things. Do you want to hear about it? I thought you would. (I love this: I get to write and you have to read. If you think about it, I've got you at this point. You could stop reading, but then you would never find out about my day. In fact, the only way you will ever know about my terrible day is to continue reading. Assuming, of course, that I do eventually get around to telling you about it. Boy, talk about a tease!) So about this famous day of mine....*

It was a dark and stormy night. Well, it was dark anyway...that's how I knew it was night. I was driving to a small town in Northern California where I was scheduled to speak. The drive took longer than I thought it would, and I ended up reaching this town (which was so small that it didn't even have a Wal-Mart! Can you imagine such a thing?) very late at night. There was only one motel in the entire place, and it was closed. Since I had few options, I slept in my truck. I tried to convince myself that it was like camping – without the campfire, marshmallows, scary stories, friends, fresh pine-scented air, or peace and quiet. OK, so it wasn't much like camping. After tossing and turning all night, I awoke to the sound of semi-trucks thundering past. I had a sore throat, and I felt like the semis were running over my head. I arrived at the school and finished the first presentation without passing out. Two minutes into the second presentation, a guy sitting in the top corner of the gym – which was packed with 1,500 people – yelled out, "Shut up, white boy!" He and his friends started laughing and joking, and the entire crowd heard him, so I knew I had to deal with the issue. I called him down on the gym floor and had him look at the audience. By the size of his eyes looking at the

* The following incidents, although real, did not all occur in the same day. These events did occur in relatively close temporal proximity, but it's a lie to say they all took place in the same 24-hour period. I realize this is somewhat deceptive. But then, life isn't fair.

size of the audience, I got the feeling he understood a little bit about my position. I said, "I think we are all agreed now on the color of my skin, aren't we?" He nodded, still looking at the audience. I asked him if he wouldn't mind paying attention for the rest of the presentation and he agreed and returned to his seat. Whew. I finished the day's presentations, and then drove to Lake Tahoe for the next day's work. A snowstorm began and, wouldn't you know it, I hit black ice. The truck skidded slowly out of control and drifted into a snowbank. As I sat in my car, I wondered if things could get worse. I knew nothing truly terrible had happened; I was still alive and healthy (except for the irritation in the back of my throat), and I even had an unopened Santa Claus Pez dispenser in my jacket pocket. But as I waited in the snow for two hours while the tow truck attempted to find my damaged car, I began to think that life was unfair *and* downright disappointing.

Most of life's disappointments are minor. Existence seems to be a series of uneventful days punctuated by the occasional major event. People do have children, get married, get divorced, graduate from high school, and die (hopefully not in that order), but life is mundane most of the time. Truly successful individuals are able to succeed in day-to-day life, accepting that life is not fair. Examples are everywhere: Michael Jordan was cut from his freshman basketball team. Tom Cruise was told he was too short to be a movie star. Fred Smith received a C on a term paper describing an overnight delivery system; then he founded a little company called Federal Express.

We face challenging situations every day. Some people see these opportunities as things that "just happen." I am beginning to learn that things rarely "just happen." More often, these situations (if we are strong enough to look at them directly) allow us to see who we are. How do you respond when something unpleasant happens in your life? Whose fault is it that you didn't get the grade you wanted on your last test, or that you didn't get the part you wanted so badly in the play? Is the world out to get you, or are you getting yourself into these situations?

Sometimes the answers to these questions are not clear-cut; we may set ourselves up for failure, but the excuses we use may also contain a nugget of truth. For example: you tried out for the lead in an upcoming school play, and you knew that you gave the best audition, but another student (who's had the lead in every school play since his freshman year) ended up getting the part. Is favoritism involved? Probably. Is that fair? Probably not. But everyone experiences this sort of injustice at some point. When I was a sophomore in high school, I thought I was a better football player than the guy who had the starting position. He had been playing that position since fifth grade though, and it was my second year. Instead of getting mad, I chose to learn from his experience. By using the tricks he taught me in tenth grade, I became the starting tight end during my senior year.

I ran for class president my freshman year in college, and

I had a ton of experience and some really solid ideas. My opponent had few ideas and even less experience. But I lost. Why? Because I forgot to campaign, to let people know about my abilities. I began to notice that, when I paid attention, life always had something to teach me.

Did you pick up on the lessons I learned from the situations listed above? Even if you did, I'll summarize them below.

1) Learn from the experience of others.

We can learn many things just by paying attention. You may think , "But wait, isn't experience the best teacher? I learn best when I do something myself!" It's true, experience *is* the best teacher. The thing about experience is that you have to make a mistake before you can learn from it, which can be a problem.

You can learn from other's experience and avoid some bad things in the first place. To use an extreme example, I have never used heroin, and I never will. Some people might say that I don't know what I am missing, but I think I do. I've met enough people who have suffered as a result of using heroin that I feel OK trusting their experience. Here's another example: Every time I leave my truck, I make sure the back is locked. Why am I so careful? Because I forgot to lock it up once, and everything in the back of the truck was stolen. How much happier I would have been if I could have learned that lesson by watching someone else. What lessons have you had to learn from experience? Are there some things you could have learned by watching other people? Are there still some lessons you have to learn the hard way?

Another good thing about paying attention is that you can learn things that you haven't had the opportunity to experience yet. What do you want to do really well? Do you know anyone who is already good at that activity, or is at least better than you? What can you learn from watching people with more experience and skill? This process is called mentoring and I think it is a lost art. Why make all the mistakes necessary to become really good at something by yourself? Doesn't it make sense to learn from someone else? I often think that there are so many mistakes to be made that I could never have enough time to make them all myself. So I learn from the mistakes of others! When I wanted to learn how to speak in public, I talked with someone who was already great, and simply asked if I could show up at his speeches. It's amazing how much you can learn from watching. I improved my speaking and learned how to critique speeches more successfully.

2) You get what you work for.

This is my mother's motto. Thank goodness we live in a democracy, where it is often true. In America, where you can achieve almost anything if you work for it, labor can be the great leveler. Some people have to work harder than others, which is unfair. It can be incredibly frustrating to watch people pick up skills without even working on them. My brother is an incredible natural athlete, and I have to work a little more. But we talked recently, and he told me that some guys on his team have even more natural ability than he does. Someone is always smarter, faster, or better looking. Don't stress about it; just focus on what you want and work towards that goal.

Do you procrastinate? Did you put this book down at least twice before you actually started reading? Do you start your homework only to hear Friends on the TV in the other room and think, "Ah, I'll get to this later." If you procrastinate even a little bit, welcome to my team. I feel like the captain of the procrastination team sometimes. It took me three days just to write that last sentence. (I'm kidding…mostly.) So how can we stop procrastinating? There a million ways: You can focus on your goal, post reminders of the tasks you want to accomplish, or write to-do lists, just to name a few possibilities. The best advice I can offer though came from Nike and, before that, my mom. Just do it. Get it done, then scratch that task off whatever list you made and go have a sundae. Yummy. But seriously, when you feel the "I-don't-want-to-do-this" bug creeping up, keep it away with "do it now" repellent.

One last word: Life still isn't fair. Even if you learn from others and work your fanny off, the girl next to you might win the lottery, which is a bummer for you. The only thing I can promise you is that you are a result of the choices you make. Winning the lottery isn't a choice, and it does little for the person inside. Working hard for something you want is a choice, and a good one. Become the person you want to be by making good choices. But still have that sundae. (smile.)

Vir~~t~~ual Valuable Reality

by
BOB LENZ

TEEN POWER *Too*

Vi~~rt~~ual Valuable Reality

by
BOB LENZ

P icture yourself in a gymnasium full of strangers. You're asked to stand up and share your most embarrassing moment. Your heart pumps faster, you feel a hot flash and a cold sweat at the same time. Your face turns as red as a Coke can and your mind goes blank. All this happens in a fraction of a second. Hey, it's okay…it's okay…you don't have to do it!

Let me share one of my most embarrassing moments with you. I was a senior at the Junior Prom. This was our last big dance in high school and we wanted to go out in style. Nine of my friends and I rented the same tuxedo – well, not the same one, but they all looked alike. In Little Chute, Wisconsin, the town I'm from, we have a tradition. We go to church before we go to prom. The ten of us sat in the front row with our dates. The pastor thought we were the prom court, so he asked us if we wanted to march out at the close of the service. We said sure, why not! So there we were, marching out of church, with our cool tuxes and dates on our arms. Pretty soon EVERYBODY thought we were the prom court...except, of course, the prom court!

When I was in high school, John Travolta was popular...the first time...not for movies like *Pulp Fiction* or *Get Shorty*, but for a movie called *Saturday Night Fever* and one called *Grease*. This was also the era of disco dancing. There we were, in the middle of the dance floor, acting like John Travolta (at least trying). Soon there was a wall of people around us yelling, "More! More! More!"

Besides pointing to the ceiling and the floor, I wondered what more did Johnny do? Then I remembered how he would jump in the air and come down doing the splits. So, I tried it. My pants went rrrrrrriiiiipppp!! This wasn't just a little rip. My pants tore from my belt buckle down to my knee. It was ventilation...big time! This would have been no big deal at a normal dance where people are scattered around the room. I could have just turned red and run. But...there was a human wall of about 50 of my classmates around me. No matter which way I turned or what I covered up, I was exposing something to someone!

I have found out since then that I am not the only one who has had an embarrassing moment. In fact, I've collected hundreds of outrageous stories that could make you laugh for hours. However, for some people their stories are not funny. I have been told, "Bob, for me it's not an embarrassing moment. I'm embarrassed about who I am."

For them, an embarrassing situation becomes a humiliating experience. From that moment of humiliation they find themselves questioning their self-worth.

What makes the difference? Why do some people walk away from a public situation and say, "That was embarrassing." Yet others walk away ashamed and say in their heart, "I am a nobody." I believe the difference comes when someone chooses to humiliate another person. You see, almost all of us have embarrassing moments. As you walk down the hall, you trip and your books go flying. What do you do? First, you brace your fall, then you look around to see if anyone saw you. If so, you nervously grin, chuckle, wave and pick up your books as your brain screams, "DA!" Later you can laugh about this and tell your friends about your most embarrassing moment.

Now consider this situation. You fall, your books go flying and you look around to see who was looking. There is a group of people laughing and pointing. One of them has his leg stuck out. You realize you've been purposely tripped. When someone chooses to hurt, humiliate, harass or degrade another human being, that individual may begin to question his or her self-worth. When we are humiliated by another person, we should realize that we have become a stepping stone for someone else's fragile self-image.

I can remember stepping on other people's self-image to build myself up. When I was in high school I was a starting player on the football team, which made me feel good. There was another guy on our team whose name was Jack (it still is). Jack wasn't good at football. I'm not putting him down, just stating a fact. He wanted to be part of the team so badly that he came to practice early and stayed late, just to fit in. You see, for some, it didn't seem okay to pursue your own talents and to be yourself. If you were a guy, you played football. That's just the way it was. Jack made the team only because the coach never cut anybody. Do you think the "starters" accepted him as part of the team? No way! We laughed at him, mocked him and used him as a blocking dummy. We had a lot of fun at his expense. One day after class, someone yelled, "Bob, look at Jack!" I turned around and saw how the other guys had hung him from the fence...by his jock strap. I hate to admit it, but I laughed uncontrollably. There he was, his arms and legs dangling from the fence. I enjoyed the prank until I walked by Jack. I saw his red face and the tears flowing down his cheeks. I thought, Jack didn't deserve that. He never did anything to hurt our team. Even if he had, we treat criminals better than that! He just wanted to belong.

The number one reason people join gangs is for a sense of belonging. Do you know what makes me sad? Some gangs would have treated Jack better than our team did. After I shared that story at a high school, the captain of the football team came up and said, "That's a powerful story but you have to finish it." "What do you mean?" I asked. "You need to tell everyone how you helped him down and became his friend," he said. I'm sorry to say that I can't do that because all of my stories are true. I knew what the other guys were doing was wrong, but I didn't help him down. I turned my head and walked by. Why? Because I chose association with the popular crowd over what I knew was right. I know now that *the right choice isn't always popular and the popular choice isn't always right.* I chose what was popular, because I didn't like who I was.

I always wanted to be like my friend, Ronny. He was good looking. That's not on my resume. I'll never make *People* Magazines' best looking man of the year. Ronny was also athletic. He could take two steps and flip. I could take 100 steps and I still couldn't flip. I do roll a little bit, though. Ronny could jump off the high dive and do whatever he wanted with his body. I jump off the high dive and the water does whatever it wants with my body. Not only was Ronny good looking and athletic, but he was the kind of guy I had a hard time with in school. I did really good in school...except for grades. Even when I did my best, the best I got was a B. *Bob – Is there something wrong with a B?* Ronny got an A even when he didn't study.

Does Ronny remind you of anyone you know? Have you ever looked to the heavens and screamed, "It's not fair! Why does this person have good looks, athletic talent and intelligence!"? If I had possessed just one of these three qualities, maybe I could have stood up and helped Jack down from the fence.

I can guarantee you that even if you have everything that society says you need to be a happy person, that doesn't assure you of a good self-image.

I found this out one night when I arrived home and found my brother, Bill, waiting for me. I knew something was wrong, "Bill, what's up?" He answered, "Bob, it's Ronny." I asked if he was okay. "Bob, Ronny is dead." I'll never forget those words and the emotion and confusion that raced through my mind. When I asked how it happened, Bill said, "Ronny got drunk and shot himself in the stomach." I was not prepared for that news. Ronny called me one of his best friends. He had it all – everything anyone could ask for.

Because of our friendship, his parents asked me to speak at his funeral. They also asked if I would go with them to identify the body. I'll never forget walking into the funeral parlor with Ronny's mom and dad on one side, and his girlfriend on the other.

In came Ronny, not with two steps and a flip, but on a cold metal cart in a blue body bag. They rolled him in front of us and unzipped the bag. There laid my friend. Lifeless. Questions raced through my mind. Why? How could Ronny not know he was valuable? How could he throw his life away? If he didn't feel significant, how could I?

My first question was answered when Ronny's mom began unloading her guilty conscience. When Ronny was young, if he did something wrong, she would hit him. She didn't spank him or discipline him. She beat him. When he was three, he spilled the milk. She went to backhand him across the face, but because he had been hit before, he put up his arm to protect himself. The back of her hand hit his elbow. She told me it stung and she lost it. She started slugging and kicking her three-year-old boy. She threw him against the wall. His body ended up so black and blue that she kept him in the house for over a month so nobody could report it to the police.

When he was seven, there were some problems in the neighborhood. The police came over. Ronny was standing by his two sisters. "Are these your children?" the officer asked his mom. She said, "These are my two girls. I don't know who that wild animal belongs to."

When he turned 11, she said he started to fight back. "I went to hit him and he grabbed my arm and said, 'Mom, no more.'" She swung the other fist at him. He grabbed that one also and yelled, "Stop!" She went ballistic and bit him on the wrist. Her teeth sunk to the bone and he had to get stitches because his own mother bit him. Can you see why Ronny thought he had no value? He was treated like trash, so he believed he was.

These were the stories she chose to tell me. I wonder how bad it was and how often it happened. Ronny never told anyone about the abuse. Maybe that was part of the problem. He pushed down the pain and hid it. But that doesn't excuse his choice to escape through suicide.

Ronny isn't the only one who has been treated without dignity. If you're not treated well, I will prove to you that no one can take away your value. If you are treated well, thank your mom and dad for loving you. Hug them and tell them you love them.

How much is a five dollar bill worth? Five dollars, of course. But what if I verbally abuse it. "You good-for-nothing five dollar bill. I wish you were never even printed. You'll never be as good as your older brother, the ten." Now, how much is it worth? Five dollars.

What if I physically abuse it by crumpling it up and throwing it on the floor. Next I step on it and spit on it. What is it worth? Five dollars. It has not lost its value.

What if I **neglect** it and stop taking it places? What if I put it in a drawer and forget about it? Does that change its value? **NO!**

If, after all this, I offered it to someone, do you think they would say, "No. I don't want it. It's been laughed at, abused and neglected. Get it away from me." Of course not! However, when those same things happen to us we begin to doubt our value.

I've seen a five dollar bill ripped into eight pieces. How much is it worth? Five dollars. You wouldn't throw it away. Why? Because it still has value!

Once I nervously took a taped five dollar bill back to the bank with a piece still missing. The teller gave me a brand new five dollar bill in exchange, and told me as long as it has the identification number on it, it has not lost its value.

Yet, when we are trashed by others, in words or actions, we doubt our self worth. When people are victims of abuse, an estimated 90% think there is something wrong with them, that somehow they deserved it. Many times they throw their lives away to drugs, alcohol, illicit sex, and other destructive choices.

Too many people end up in the landfill of regret. This can stop by knowing and remembering that you are valuable. You are more than a number. You are a human being with a unique identity. You have rights and value that can never, ever be taken away.

The Declaration of Independence says, "We hold these truths to be self-evident, that all men (people) are created equal. That they are endowed by their Creator with certain unalienable rights, that among these are life, liberty and the pursuit of happiness."

You are worth so much more than a five dollar bill. The

five dollar bill has value, even torn, because it has a government inscription, a number and a seal. The government stands behind it and verifies its value.

Our Creator has put His characteristic marks on you. He has made you in His image, male and female. He will stand beside you and never leave you. He says, "I vouch for you, I created you. I don't care what you've done or how you've been treated. I love you! You have value." Our Creator has a plan and a purpose for each and every person. You are not trash. Believe God's opinion of you.

Value-Based Actions

1. Just as I gave the ripped up five dollar bill back to the bank, give your heart and all its pieces back to the One who made you.

2. If you are a victim, talk to somebody. Break the silence. Get help.

3. Surround yourself with people who will affirm your dignity and treat you with respect.

4. Remember and believe that just because you are *treated* like trash, doesn't *make* you trash.

5. Make choices based on your value, not on how others treat you.

6. Choose to treat others with dignity and respect.

7. Let your words and actions declare the value of every human being.

ME,
The Perfect Date?

by
ELLEN MARIE

TEEN POWER
Too

ME, The Perfect Date?

by

ELLEN MARIE

There she was, the most beautiful girl in the school. She was standing with her friends by the dance floor while a slow song began playing. Maybe you get the courage to ask her to dance, and she looks you right in the eye and says "Nope." That's it. No excuse, no explanation, just a plain "Nope." As you return to your spot near the wall, your "friends" are laughing because you got rejected, again. So you tell yourself, "I don't care, I was just doing her a favor anyway. She looked lonely."

Rejection, Rejection, Rejection.

Well, if you choose to date, everyone goes through rejection at some time. What's sad is many people think just because one person, (or maybe three or four,) doesn't want to date them, that no one will ever want to date them. When we take the risk to begin dating, we must accept that not every person will be right.

Breaking up is normal. Look at it this way: if you never broke up with anyone, and no one ever broke up with you, then you would marry the first person you dated. Eekk! For some of us that is a scary thought. We have grown and changed so much since our first date.

The next time you feel sad, rejected or unloved, let me suggest you do this: ask at least five married adults, (perhaps your aunts, uncles, parents, neighbors, or grandparents) how old they were when they met their current spouse. Be sure to ask at least three couples under the age of 35, because it was more common to marry young when your grandparents were teenagers.

Do you ever think maybe the best person for you will be someone you meet in college, vocational school, or on your first job? Give relationships time to develop and do not try to control the other person. Many of you will not marry someone you meet in high school, but some will. Some may not date in high school. Therefore, the years before you meet "the one" (or make a commitment to this person) should be used for self-discovery and to make yourself a better date or a better potential mate.

So let's get started!!

BE TRUE TO YOU

OK, you've heard this one before, but it is so true. BE YOURSELF!! What I mean by this is don't try to change your personality to fit what you think your date wants you to be. If you think you should be as charming and romantic as Romeo or Juliet, as attractive as a Brad Pitt or Cindy Crawford, or witty as a Will Smith, get real! If you believe your date wants to be with someone super funny, (but no one has ever laughed with you, only at you), you may be putting too high expectations on yourself. On the other hand, if your date expects things from you that don't fit your personality, then you may not be with the best match. This is not to say that being kind, fun, good looking and an interesting conversationalist are not attractive qualities, they are. However, the point is to develop what you already have, do not be someone you are not. I'm going to present some ideas anyone can use to develop into a better date. Fit them into your already existing personality, and be the best YOU can be.

HE SAID/SHE SAID

Have you ever been on a date and your mouth didn't work? When you're with your friends you often have lots to talk about, right? But with a date, NOTHING. After you talk about weather what else is there? In his book, "How To Win Friends And Influence People," Dale Carnegie said many years ago, "You can make more friends in two months by becoming interested in other people than you can in two years by trying to get other people interested in you" (p.74). In other words, be more interested in the other person, than in yourself. Ask your dates about themselves. For example: • how many brothers or sisters they have • what they do for hobbies • were they ever a boy/girl scout • how they get along with their parents • if they could do any job, what it would be • if they could travel anyplace, where would it be • who is their favorite musician/actor • what teacher they like/dislike • do they believe in God • how important is their faith to them • where were they born.

Not only will your dates be pleased you have taken such an interest in them, but you will learn a lot about who they are and what they believe. The more you know about your dates, the better you can determine if you share similar interests. Furthermore, the more you develop your own interests and know yourself, you can more clearly define who will be the best match for you.

Another way to get to know your dates better is to do activities that bring about conversation and shared interests. For example, most people go to a movie the first few dates. Although a movie is entertaining, it gives little time to get to know the other person.

The following are some activities that will stimulate conversation and make your time together unique: • go to the fair • make your date dinner • go window shopping for expensive things you can't buy, but just wish for • go shopping for music • go to a museum • play board games or cards • have a picnic • play pool or darts • go bowling and make bets who will treat for dinner etc. • go for a walk in a park • have a snowball fight (for those in cold climates like Minnesota) • go to the beach (for those of you in more favorable climates) • wash each other's car • have a water balloon fight • play with a dog/cat • go horseback riding • play Nintendo • go out for ice-cream and a walk • fly a kite • go downhill skiing • look through old photo albums • go to a sporting event • make cookies • go out with a group of at least four people to help stimulate the conversation • ask for the next date by a romantic letter, or send a thank you card for the date. These things may sound unusual, but I bet you'll remember your time together and learn a lot about each other. And isn't that what dating is all about? A main purpose of dating is to help you choose the type of person best suited for you. Remember, when you're on dates, introduce your date to your friends or family; don't leave them out of conversations; look them in the eye when speaking and smile at them. They like that.

Doing the kinds of activities listed above can also help avoid the temptation of developing the relationship on sex rather than on each other's personality. A solid relationship needs a foundation of friendship, respect, and trust. Furthermore, a relationship should **add** to your life, but not dominate it. Some people believe that once they've found Mr. or Ms. Right, they need to spend every moment with each other. Although this may be tempting, do not drop your friends!! You will still need them. Even though everything looks promising now, don't burn the bridges of your friendships. Friends can give you another perspective on your relationship.

A friend told me she was madly in love with her date of only a short time. She said they were having sexual intercourse and she knew this was the "one." So I asked, "what do you like about him?" "What?" she responded. I repeated the question. Then she asked, "What do you mean, what do I like about him?" she looked puzzled. "Well" I responded, "If you 'love' him, you must 'like' something about him." She responded, "I don't know, I guess he's nice." A few years after that conversation, she married another man.

Please understand: Good sex does not equal a good relationship.

If you want to know if a relationship is solid, don't have sex, and see how long the relationship lasts. You will be more likely to develop the relationship on qualities such as friendship, respect, trust, shared interests, conversation and other things that keep relationships alive. Sex will be something you can both look forward to. The purpose of dating is to learn to relate, not mate. Remember, dating helps you choose the type of person best suited for you. Having sexual intercourse can confuse this process. The focus can switch from who you are personally, to what each person receives physically. In addition, there are incurable sexually transmitted diseases to be concerned about.

After I presented my program "Reality in Relationships"

to a group of teenagers, a girl asked me this question. She said "What does your boyfriend think about not having sex. I've heard a lot of guys talk about it and they think it is stupid to wait and that girls are stupid who want to wait." Deciding to be sexually abstinent, or making any choice that prevents consequences YOU have to live with, is NOT stupid. Making good choices is sign of maturity and adulthood. Making wise choices can give a person freedom. By being sexually abstinent, a person avoids sexually transmitted diseases, unwanted pregnancy, sexual comparisons with a future spouse and emotional consequences. Waiting to be sexually active can be a choice, even if you've already had sex. This decision takes self-control, honest communication and a commitment before the date begins.

Recently I was the director of a crisis pregnancy center near the University of Minnesota. I remember a college freshman who came for a pregnancy test after having been with her ex-boyfriend. Before the test results were completed, I asked her if she had ever thought of practicing sexual abstinence. She told me she had planned to be abstinent until marriage, but got drunk one night and lost her virginity. She then went on to say she figured now there was no reason to wait. That day, the pregnancy test came back positive.

It is never too late to change any behavior that may result in consequences you aren't ready to handle.

A few years ago while living in Fargo, ND, I decided to try skydiving. It was something I had always wanted to do and a friend of mine had just learned. I took a hands-on course and on the third day was ready for the jump. The course trained me on all the precautions and made me practice what I would do should my parachute not open. I assumed this would never happen to me. There were six skydivers in our plane along with the jumpmaster. The first several times a person skydives, the jumpmaster attaches a rope to the parachute cord and pull it for the skydiver. This is called a static-line jump and is done in case the rookie jumper panics and forgets to pull the shoot. I remember dropping from the plane as if it was yesterday. Within 3 seconds the jumpmaster pulled my parachute cord and my shoot was above my head. However, it wasn't opening. My parachute lines were twisted and I was dropping fast. My immediate response was panic, but within 5 seconds I said to myself, "Ellen, you know exactly what to do. You prepared for this situation many times. Just relax and follow through on what you've learned." I did just that and landed safely to the ground.

The point of this true story is to illustrate the importance of being prepared in advance for a pressure situation. You also can prepare in advance for what you may do if someone pressures you to do something you know will be harmful to your future. The important thing is to know what your values are and where you will draw the line, before you are in a tough situation. It is always easier to deal with situations when you've decided in advance what you will do.

After two separate high school assembly programs, a female and male high school student approached me with the same concern. "If I don't have sex with my date, they will break up with me. What should I do?" I told them, "If someone demands that you do what they want, and you are put at risk just to keep them...you never had them in the first place." Real love is not based on sex or doing what the other wants. Real love is wanting what is <u>best</u> for the other person. Below are some qualities that separate love from infatuation. Check which fit your current relationship or a relationship you want to have.

LOVE VS INFATUATION

Love Tends To Be:

- Based on wanting what is best for the other person

- Built on many aspects of the other person, not just one.

- Respecting each other and admiring unique qualities.

- Strengthened by acceptance of the person's weaknesses.

- Increasing, even with no sexual activity.

- Strengthened by physical attraction to the other person, combined with an attraction to his or her heart, mind and personality.

- When many of your friends and family agree this person is good for you.

- Developed through shared interests and activities.

- Built on trust and free from intense jealousy.

Infatuation Tends To Be:

- Focused on few traits, usually physical ones.

- Filled with insecurity which forces people to do things they would not normally do just to keep the relationship.

- Associated with little growth in the relationship over time.

- Full of overlooked or avoided problems in order to keep the relationship together.

- Filled with constant jealousy and mistrust.

- Based on going out with someone so others see you dating him/her.

- Revolved entirely around sex, so much so that any other activities seem boring.

- Signified by being someone they are not, in order to keep the relationship.

What type of a relationship do you have? What type do you want? What are you doing to make yourself the type of person others want to date? If your relationship is not all it can be, try to make it better. If that doesn't work, be honest with yourself when in an unhealthy relationship and move on.

You deserve the right relationship for you.

Remember, rather than look for a perfect date or mate, develop yourself to be a better date. Starting today!!

10 Seconds…
Can Change Your
Life Forever!

by
BOBBY PETROCELLI

10 Seconds…Can Change Your Life Forever!

by
BOBBY PETROCELLI

1. 2. 3. 4. 5. 6. 7. 8. 9. 10. Now repeat what you just read aloud. All it took was 10 seconds to read it again. That short amount of time can impact your life and our entire world forever.

Everything that happens and every decision we make, occurs within a 10 second time frame. The reality of this hit home (literally), while I was living through a horrible tragedy – a drunk driver crashing through your house while you and your wife are asleep in bed, will definitely impact your life forever.

According to an eyewitness and the police who were at the scene, a 35 year old male driving his light blue & white Ford f-150 full-size 4 x 4 pickup truck was "gunning it" as he drove into my housing development. The truck, out of control, hit the concrete dividing median, traveled over the median, and into the two exiting lanes where it was now driving on the wrong side of the road for about 30 feet. Then, it crossed back over the median, across the incoming lanes. The full-size ton pickup truck hit the far side curb, drove over it, and rode up onto the grassy field that proceeded my beautiful ranch-style brick home.

The truck sped across the grassy field, traveling a distance of 313 feet, continuing on a direct path heading straight toward my back brick bedroom wall, which was located on the side of my house. Judging by the distance it traveled, it was estimated that the truck was traveling approximately 70 miles an hour as it crashed through my bedroom wall. I was sleeping 5 feet from the brick wall.

The truck ran over me completely as the spinning tires burned rubber into my body. I was then somehow flipped onto the hood of the truck – carried through the inside bedroom wall and deposited into the dining room window. I awoke sitting in a slumped position, as my wife Ava, entangled in the sheets and mattress, was buried underneath the truck.

The paramedics told us that Ava was so enmeshed in the rubble, it took them over 20 minutes to free her. When they finally reached her, she was dead. The cause of death– asphyxia due to suffocation. You can't even imagine the devastation this brought to so many. **Tragedies steal, kill and destroy!**

Two things dawned on me more than ever – first, this

could have been prevented. The man driving the pickup truck had a blood alcohol content of almost .19. In most states he would be considered double legally drunk. Secondly, this tragedy could not have taken more than 10 seconds to occur.

When a vehicle is traveling 70 miles per hour, it is moving approximately 104 feet per second. It only took 3 seconds for the truck to travel 313 feet across the grassy field. Add 3 or 4 seconds when the driver first entered my housing development. All it took was 6-7 seconds for the truck to reach my brick bedroom wall. Add 3-4 seconds when the truck crashed through my wall and finally came to a halt in my living room. *__10 seconds is all it took to change my life forever!__*

Then it occurred to me, the decision the man made to drive under the influence probably took him no more than 10 seconds to make. I now realized it was not the decision he made that fatal night that changed my life forever, though that is true – but it was every decision he made in his life, starting with the first drink he took in high school, until the last drink he took that night, at 35 years old – and then got in his truck and drove – that finally caught up to him.

I know you've heard the expression, "what goes around comes around and what you sow you are going to reap." We have been created with the greatest gift of all, the freedom of choice – *__Not the freedom of consequences__*. Every decision we make, whether good or bad, effects everyone.

In 1992 I had the privilege of beginning an exotic three day cruise vacation throughout the Bahamas. The awesome sunsets, the crystal blue water and the joys of a relaxing vacation. Unexpectedly, my three-day cruise turned into a five-day adventure because we were being chased by the most devastating and costly hurricane in American history. Hurricane Andrew was packing winds clocked at 165 mph as it made landfall in Homestead, Florida.

When we returned, the destruction was catastrophic. Housing developments lay in ruin and lives were left in chaos. Then I noticed something that struck me – in the midst of the devastation, the only thing left intact – was the foundation of each building. Regardless of the storms' devastating power – all you could see for miles – was row after row of concrete foundations.

I began to understand an even greater truth – as long as our lives foundation is strong enough, we have the ability to weather any storm. If the house of our life is destroyed– when our foundation is stable – we can clean the rubble away – and start to rebuild the house all over again. Usually bigger and better than ever.

As I continued to meditate on this, I reached the conclusion – we build the foundation of our life, 1 brick, 1 decision – 10 seconds at a time.

The weak foundation that the drunk driver built for himself, finally led to his demise. My foundation ultimately helped me to triumph over tragedy.

Choosing "to be better" and not bitter was not an easy task. Relying on the "three F's" of my foundation was of utmost importance – faith, forgiveness and family/friends.

Having the faith to trust in God, more than ever, would be an incredible challenge. True faith is not faith, until you "go through the fire" and still believe.

I knew I had to forgive because unforgiveness would've stopped me from pressing on with my life. Many people have the misconception that unforgiveness gets back at the person who hurt them. Unforgiveness hinders us from being the best we could be. *"I forgive you,"* are the three greatest words you can ever say. Don't forget that you might've done something to hurt someone else and desire their forgiveness.

Trusting in family and friends for support and encouragement was essential. My supporting cast helped me stand strong and not give up. They were with me every step of the way.

We set patterns, habits and routines that either lead us

towards one of two directions: triumph or tragedy. In every decision we make we are planting seeds. These seeds will one day bring forth a harvest. We all plant both flower seeds and weed seeds. I would rather plant more flower seeds and less weeds. I would rather reach for the top and just miss than reach for the middle and make it. By reaching for the top and just missing, will still put you so far ahead than just settling for being mediocre.

Whatever we put our time into, that is what we will be successful in. Tomorrow, we will either benefit from or pay for the lives we live today. ***Things don't just happen!.*** Things happen because of the foundation everyone builds – 1 brick 1 decision, 10 seconds at a time. What we put into it, is what we will get out of it. "What goes around comes around, what we sow we will reap."

Three and-a-half years after my tragedy, I had the privilege of being remarried. And I don't mind telling you – I married the most beautiful flower on this earth – my wife Suzanne Marie. We are blessed with two of the most precious gifts, my two sons: Alec Robert and Aron James. (And they both look just like their Daddy!)

During the darkest days of my tragedy, little did I know how blessed I would be. I am so glad I held onto faith, hope and love. To top it off, I am doing what I love to do. I am having the honor and opportunity of sharing my story with millions of people worldwide. My friends always joke with me because they know how much I love to talk.

It's always a privilege sharing my life with young people. Recently, I had spoken to over 1000 students in a high school assembly in Louisiana. When I finished speaking, I was mobbed by students who wanted to talk with me. This is always my favorite time of the program because I get to share one on one.

As a young lady approached me, I noticed she was crying. She introduced herself and said, "Bobby, I want to thank you for such a wonderful program and to tell you that after all these years, it is such a privilege for me to finally meet you." I pondered, "How does she know me?"

She continued, "I remember when you experienced your tragedy. One evening during dinner, while my family and I were watching the evening news, your story was featured. I mentioned to my parents that we needed to pray for Bobby Petrocelli. The reason that I am so excited today – 10 years ago, while I was a kindergarten student, I prayed for a man I didn't even know. It's so awesome that my prayers have had an impact on your recovery. I have a part in what you are doing today. To top it off, you came to speak at my high school. I realize more than ever how every 10 second decision and action affects all of us."

By the time she finished talking, that precious blonde-haired high school junior was not the only person crying and being thankful.

You have probably heard the expression "Carpe diem" used

before. It means to "Seize the day." The actor Robin Williams made this expression famous in the movie "Dead Poets Society." It's a great motto that many people live by.

Personally, I'd rather utilize the motto I made up, "Carpe momento" or "Carpe 10 secondaro." In another words, you cannot get through the day or "Seize the day" until you "Seize the moment" or "Seize the 10 seconds." When you live moment to moment, 10 seconds to 10 seconds, you eventually complete the day. Everything that takes place in our world happens moment by moment, ten seconds at a time.

When people are in the midst of a difficult situation, the big picture often seems overwhelming. If they can work through the moment or 10 seconds, they may feel they have accomplished something. Step by step, moment by moment, 10 seconds at a time.

To work towards your ultimate goal, first deal with the moment – then 10 seconds – then 1 minute – the hour, and before you know you will have seized the day, the week, the month, the year, the decade – and finally the lifetime.

Realize that you are always in control of your own actions, reactions and responses. You have no control over how others treat and react towards you. You can't change others if they don't want to change. Work at changing and improving yourself.

I had no control over the fact that the drunk driver crashed through my house, killed my wife, never apologized to me – or that he only served 4 months in jail. However, I did have control over how I would respond to the situation. Though the drunk driver brought tragedy into my life – a greater tragedy would have been if I chose not to continue with my life.

In all your relationships, you are not responsible for other people's actions. You <u>are</u> responsible for the way you act, react and respond. **There can't be any excuses!** No ifs, ands, or but's! ***<u>You control your decisions!</u>*** It only takes 10 seconds to say, "Thank you" or "I love you" or "I forgive you." ***<u>Treat others the way you want to be treated!</u>***

Make a strong stand for your beliefs, don't let others influence you to make wrong decisions. There is a very slim chance that very many of those who are in your life today, will even be in your life in the future

Let me give you an example – I attended a Brooklyn, New York high school of 3500 students. I was well-liked, an athlete, and known by many students. Once I walked out those doors for graduation, there was only one friend that I still kept in touch with. Why?

Our lives go in different directions – some go to college, some go into the military, some get married, move away – etc. Ask any adult – the fact of the matter is, we are willing to put our faith, hope and love in people who are in our lives today, when there's a good chance that they won't even be in our lives in the future.

We make many life changing decisions based on the influence of friends who are presently active in our lives. We become so entangled by impressing others and often allow them to influence us to make foolish 10 second life altering decisions.

Of the 4500 students that I attended Oral Roberts University with, only a handful are active in my life today. I consider them my closest friends.

Friends can be compared to an elevator button, they are either going to bring you up or bring you down.

When I needed them most, my true friends were there for me. Adversity can bring out the best in people and reveal who your true friends are.

Whenever I return home from a trip, it brings me such joy to be greeted by my wife and children. My son Alec always says, "Daddy, I love you and I miss you so much – what surprise did you bring me, Daddy?"

I always ask Alec if he was a good boy. Usually he tells me that he was. Once, when he was 3 years old, he started to confess the sins he committed while I was away. Tearfully he said, "Daddy, last night while Mommy was giving me a bath (then halfway through the story he laughs and smiles) – I threw the telephone in the bath tub! Daddy, you are going to have to fix it, or buy a new one."

Like most Italians, I begin talking to Alec vigorously using my hands.(Do you know why Italians talk with their hands? It's because we spit so much when we talk – we try to catch all the spit with our hands before it lands on the people we're talking to.)

"Alec, you can't throw the telephone in the tub because you can't always fix it or afford to buy a new one." What I was really saying – was that in life, some things can never be fixed or replaced.

Though some things can never be fixed or replaced – it's never too late to fix or rebuild your life's foundation. *It's only 1 brick, 1 decision, 10 seconds away.*

When I was younger, I always wanted to play professional baseball like my uncle Rico Petrocelli, who played for the Boston Red Sox. Even though I was a good player, I never reached that goal because I couldn't hit the curve ball.

When life threw me a curveball, I hit that curveball so far – the ball is still traveling today. When life throws you a curveball, and trust me, it will – will the strength of your life's foundation prepare you to hit it?

Whatever you put your time into, that's what you will be successful in. Make your life count, make a difference and make the change that you need to – 1 brick, 1 decision at a time.

My goal for you in life is that you always find *faith, hope and love*...10 seconds at a time!

Mind
The Magic Wand

by
JeVon Thompson

TEEN
POWER
Too!

Mind
The Magic Wand
by
JEVON THOMPSON

"Zorro Explains Stupid and Ignorant"

I was raised by my grandmother. Bessie Rowe was an old black woman from the south. She lived to be 104, and believe me, Bessie "didn't take no stuff." In her seventies she was an agile opponent for anyone. She walked with a cane and was skillful with it. I lovingly called her Zorro, but only behind her back, of course. Up front she was Gram.

I got in trouble at school once. In those days that was sure death, especially if the school called home. It was an embarrassment to the family, a sign of "po up-bring." Old black folk, especially those from southern traditions, didn't tolerate it.

Bessie sat at the table with a fixed glare. "Now listen. You's a good kid and I love ya with all my heart, but sometime you act stupid and ignorant."

"Gram, everybody makes mistakes."

"That's right. And I don't have a problem with that. I do have a problem with stupid and ignorant."

"Well…how do you mean, Gram? I don't think I can be both at the same time, can I?"

"Today you was. Them same boys in trouble all the time and you just had to be with 'em all of a sudden. You never played with them kind before."

"I know, Gram. I really don't even like most of them, but they were hard to avoid today." It was the truth. However, she was absolutely right. This group never seem to learn from their mistakes. "Gram, what's ignorant?"

She sat up a little and pursed her lips. "Boy, ignorant is when you dumb and you don't know you dumb and that how dumb you is."

"When I don't know something."

"Yes."

"What's stupid, then?"

"That's easy. Stupid is when you do something dumb and you know I'm gonna be after you with this cane, and you do it anyway. That's stupid." She paused and looked at me with clear eyes. "Now which one you think is worse?"

"Stupid," I said without hesitation.

Seriousness lined her face. "No. Ignorant. When you dumb and don't know you dumb, you can't fix it. Then dumb becomes normal, like them boys." She allowed me to sit in silence until I got it. I nodded.

We all need a wake-up call on an act of ignorance or stupidity now and then so we can learn from our mistakes, but most of us have heard how stupid we are too many times. We learn to use this against ourselves, automatically limiting our lives.

"Elephants?"

Limited thinking: "I can't" or self-directed negative thought: "I'm stupid," makes our lives less than they could be. If you had an elephant in your kitchen you couldn't turn out a great meal. There would be no room for your own greatness. If your mind is embedded with thoughts of unworthiness, filled with doubts about your own abilities and stymied by fear, you can't create a feast of successful living.

Thoughts don't have to be "real" or "true" to create failure or success in our life. They just have to be believed. The more emotion invested, the more real it becomes – for you. A thought in which you believe with deep feelings will be a powerful catalyst in your life.

You stand and stare at a water choked sink and know that somewhere, beyond your scope of vision, the drain is clogged. Your guess is as good as mine, but we're probably talking about a mesh of hairballs wadded in soap scum and old tooth paste, a plastic eyelash, some old dental floss, stuff unthinkable to touch even if it is yours. But it's down there taking on a life of its own. The clog, in a small way, has made your life more difficult and less fun. If you ignore it long enough you stop noticing it as a problem. You incorporate it into your life.

Negative thinking and limited thoughts clog you up. False or negative thoughts control lives and create behaviors that you might not even see because they appear "normal." People see us and wonder why we don't change the behaviors that appear like elephants in our kitchens.

Elephant diet: Try a thirty-day-no-negative-thinking (about yourself or others) diet.

No one is born with negative beliefs about themselves. These self-defeating ideas come initially from outside sources, often from people who are on a mission to convince you that you have the same problems that they do. Why? "Misery loves company." They have so many elephants squashing their dreams, they just drop by to see if you could use a few.

Other, more insidious, false or negative, thoughts come directly and intentionally from sources that stand to gain something from controlling how you think. They reach you through the media and subtly let you know there's something wrong with you. The sale of beauty products is a billion dollar business. The cosmetic industry has to convince you that your body is plagued: ugly, blotched, wrinkled, dried up, and abnormally pimpled.

Next, they have to convince you they have the answer – for a price. This war is fought on the battleground of your minds. The winners get to put your money into their banks.

To our own peril, we have all had someone else think for us. In 1970 my fashion vision got short-circuited. I went through a phase that looked like "Jimi Hendrix snorts Draino with George 'P. Funk' Clinton." I wore orange platform shoes, orange and white checked socks, orange crush velvet pants, a billowy sleeve shirt, one very large heavy medallion and a huge afro with a part down the middle. I didn't have any goldfish in my platforms, but I don't think that alone will clear my good name. There you have it.

We allow ourselves to be manipulated at every turn by friends, school cliques, television, radio, magazines, the clothing, cosmetics, and fast food industries. How often during the course of a day do you really think your own thoughts when you are constantly having your sense of well-being attached to the images of cars, perfumes or certain brands of cigarettes? To replace limited negative thinking with positive growth-producing thinking, we need to do things a different way.

"We All Dumb In Math"

My family members were great conversationalist around the dinner table. Certain subjects came up with regularity. One in particular was that some members of my family, yours truly included, were dumb in math beyond hope. I always heard my name on the end of the family list of mathematically impaired. After fourteen years of this I began to accept it as indisputable and unchangeable fact. In high school I failed algebra three times. Eventually I passed and was accepted to a college in Wisconsin where I applied for a psychology degree. One small problem stood between me and my degree – statistics. It was a four-hour lab which had to be taken in my junior year. After hearing all the horror stories circulating about statistics, I mentally went into the fetal position. The panic was overwhelming.

One day I was called to my professor's office. Professor Fine, a short, stout man with thinning hair and a perpetual smile, sat on the front of his desk with his feet dangling off the floor. He read my transcript and held up his hands over his head. "My son, this is your lucky day."

I looked up. He repeated, "This is indeed your lucky day.

This is where all of your tenacity pays off. You're going to be great in stats." He had a huge smile on his face.

"How's that, Doc?" I asked.

He shrugged. "You have the second kind of mind. Listen. 'First kind of minds' are the kids who do well in algebra, but don't get stats. They struggle like crazy in stats. It's a different kind of math that takes a different kind of mind. 'Second kind of mind' is like yours." He held up my grades. "Didn't have a clue about algebra, but you'll probably get an A in stats. Kids who get algebra, *don't* get stats. Kids who don't get algebra understand statistics with no problem. If you failed algebra once, I'd guess you'd get an A or a B in stats. Think about it, son. You flunked three times. You're gonna be a genius." He raised his hands over his head again. Eureka!

"Really?" I asked, confused.

He jumped to the floor and held my face with his free hand and looked me square in the eyes. "Really. And I'm happy for you. You never gave up and now it's going to pay off."

I was ecstatic with the news. He tossed my transcript on the floor near the trash can, shook my hand, and slapped my back with great enthusiasm. As I left the old ivy-covered brick building and started across the campus, I looked up to the second floor window. Professor Fine was smiling, holding up two fingers for "second kind of mind." I smiled back and held up three fingers for "flunked three times." This scene was repeated a thousand times until I reached my junior year. Each and every time there was a smile of approval on his face, a firm and enthusiastic handshake, perhaps an introduction to another professor during which glowing expectations were recounted.

Eventually I began to tell my friends how well I expected to do in statistics. This singular change in attitude/mind affected all my grades. With the awareness of my new "second kind of mind" I received the best grades of my life in college. I never believed I would do that well and probably wouldn't have if it had not been for professor Fine's intercession.

For two years I looked forward to taking statistics. When the time finally arrived, I did something that I had never done in any other math class – I fought for a front row seat. I asked so many questions I was often called a pest. My statistics book was never very far from me that semester. Also, there was little time for friends and hanging out. I set priorities and stuck to them.

Despite what the professor had said, it was hard work and took concentration and an occasional tutor. It paid off. I received one of only a handful of A's that year. Shortly after, I ran into one of the professors former aides who said, "Congratulations. Professor Fine tells his really slow students that second-kind-of-mind story." And then he looked at me and said, "Hmm. You'd be surprised how often it works. The mind is amazing isn't it?"

The brain is extraordinary. In today's computer terms, think of it as hardware. Negative thoughts can be like big, lumbering elephants that slow you down while other, more positive, thought programs help you to soar like an eagle.

> Your belief charged with emotion is the power source that makes it all happen.

"AHA!"

Professor Fine introduced me to his daughter Terri and we became great friends. I remember her being very intelligent and challenging in discussions. Terri's mind was like a pinball, excitingly bouncing off one idea and then another, gaining momentum until she finally hit the jackpot with an AHA! experience.

On the other hand, I can be a little slow at times. Often I have to walk away from an idea and sit for a while before my "AHA!" clicks on.

Sometimes it takes years before the "AHA!" rolls over some of us like an avalanche on a Colorado ski slope.

One warm and humid fall day in 1973, I came out of the old ivy-covered building that housed the professor's office and saw Terri sitting cross-legged on the grass. She sat absently rubbing on perfumed hand lotion while staring at nothing in particular, obviously grinding ideas.

I plopped down next to her and off we went chasing first one thought and then another. After about an hour she got up to leave. As she walked away she turned and topped her last argument by saying, "Why do you insist that it would be so impossible? We all have the same brain that Einstein had, you know." She hesitated for a moment searching my face for lights. Seeing none, she chuckled and walked away.

"Einstein's brain. Yeah right," I laughed.

Years later I was giving a seminar on unlimited thinking. It was a great group of students who had no problem exploring the possibilities – with one exception. One young man who felt certain that he would be as his father was, who was like his father before him. And he wasn't very hopeful or happy about it.

I went after the elephant in his kitchen with everything I had. The elephant had been well entrenched since childhood, the pet of an alcoholic father and a grandfather who, from what the young man said, had never given him one word of praise or encouragement. His elephant seemed more lethal than my "dumb-in-math" pachyderm. He persisted.

Finally I said, "We may want other people to love, praise and accept us, but in real life we can't control that. Perhaps you should tell yourself that you're ok. Don't wait for someone else to do it. It may never come. You know, we all have the same brain that Einstein had." I fell silent. My eyes shot up to the back of my head searching for memories. The muggy fall afternoon came flooding back – the ivy, the heat, the fragrance of Terri's hand lotion and…then the avalanche: "AHA! That's what she meant."

I was lost in space with wonderful memories. Finally a voice broke into my bubble. It was the big guy sitting in front of me. "I've been waiting all my life. Maybe, I better get on with it."

And then another voice from somewhere else in the room said, "Yeah. Me too." Both of them had an "AHA!" and both of them kicked elephants out of the kitchen – elephants that had been sitting on their dreams.

Once you return all the elephants of limited thinking to their rightful owners and begin to refuse new ones, you have a chance to use your mind as it is intended: to create a future that makes you excited and fills you with antici-pation. Temporary ignorance and an occasional act of stupidity are normal parts of growing up, but to allow outside sources to continually fill you with limiting thoughts that slowly become your own is perilous at best. Your mind is flexible and obedient, and knows no bound-aries except for those you embrace. You must passionately take control of your own mental magic wand. For those who believe, this is possible. Anything is possible.

The Equation
For Love

by
S<small>USIE</small> V<small>ANDERLIP</small>

TEEN
POWER
Too

The Equation For Love

by
<u>Susie Vanderlip</u>

D o you stand in front of the mirror in the morning and say to yourself:

"My nose is TOO big!!!"

"My hair looks awful!!"

"I've got a zit! No way I can go to school!"

"If only I was taller…blonder…bigger…."

"If only, IF only, IF ONLY!"

Or have you ever thought:

"I'm not smart enough."

"I'm too stupid."

"I'm too fat, too ugly, too sensitive, too SOME-THING! Nobody will ever like me."

"I can't get into that college."

"I'll never get a good job."

Whatever!! "I'm NOT GOOD ENOUGH!"

"Whatever" your head says you are or are not, I guarantee

you, someone else's head has said it too. More often than not, it isn't true! Your own head can beat you up far worse than even your worst enemy!

Like many kids, I grew up with nicknames, some good, some not so good. My mom lovingly referred to me as her "little peanut" and "mighty mouse." I'm only 5'0" tall, but she sees me as capable and full of driving idealism. However, my mom also called me "worry-wart" and my dad called me "too sensitive." To some people, I was "too short," "too smart," "too something." As a result, I began to think I was not "good enough" at a very young age, no matter how much I accomplished.

As a child (and as an adult, too!) I wanted lots of love and affection. However, as a child I didn't know how to ask for it. I lived in a busy household of four kids, two dogs, a cat, turtle, birds, hamsters, mice, fish, ducks, a mom and dad. I did not understand busy parents; I just understood I wanted to be loved. As a very young child I concluded, "I have to compete for attention and affection. I have to <u>earn</u> love."

Today, as an adult, I know that it is healthy to ask for attention, hugs, and someone to listen when I need to talk. I know that it is healthy to ask for what I need. However, as a child at three, five, eight, twelve, and even fifteen, I <u>ASSUME</u>d that to be loved, I had to <u>do</u> something, <u>accomplish</u> something, <u>be worthy</u> of attention, affection and love.

What does all that have to do with waking up and picking on your nose, your hair, your body, or your personality as a teen? Well, I ASSUMEd at the age of three that I had to earn love. That simple ASSUMPTION stuck in my brain. This one belief became the hidden motive for many choices I made in my teens and even later as an adult.

I've learned the hard way that the things we ASSUME when very young determine how we think about ourselves for a long, long time!

Think about it, if we believe that we must <u>do something</u> to receive love and affection, but don't know what that something is, we'll try to do everything right, right?! and hope that something works. We may become The Perfectionist, harshly critical of ourselves, cruelly comparing ourselves to others, picking on ourselves in every mirror! Or, we may become The Rebel, saying, "Who cares, anyway!" and head down a path of dangerous choices and painful consequences.

The one ASSUMPTION that we are not good enough makes it difficult to experience joy in life, may make us push ourselves beyond reasonable limits, become judgemental of ourselves and others, or become self-destructive.

We <u>all</u> want to be loved. We may be angry and deny it, but deep down we need love in our lives to be healthy.

I met a seventeen-year-old girl recently named Natalie.

She had a boyfriend, about twenty-one years old. Her mother didn't like her daughter dating an older boy. Natalie began by saying she didn't care what her mother thought. Natalie was sneaking out of the house and skipping school to be with him. She felt that school was stupid and so were her parents. Why should she talk to them or any other adult, for that matter.

I just listened. I began to hear what sounded familiar. I heard her hidden motives, the things she had ASSUMEd about love in her family. You see, we all learn about love, both the good and the bad, from our families when we are children. So I asked Natalie, "Did you and your mom talk <u>before</u> you met your boyfriend?"

"Yeah," Natalie said. "In fact, we used to be like good friends, but now, she just tells me I'm stupid and ruining my life. So, I don't talk to her any more."

"Did you and your mom have a fight when you first met your boyfriend?" I asked. And here is where I heard what she had ASSUMEd about love in her family, the thoughts that were now causing her to make dangerous and troubling choices.

"Well, my mom came into my room one night," Natalie began hesitantly, "and she found me with my boyfriend. We weren't doing anything, but, well, I think my mom lost respect for me. And we haven't talked since."

Natalie had been a good student and a great softball player before this incident. Now she had ASSUMEd her mother was ashamed of her and could not possibly love her the same any more. Natalie ASSUMEd when very young that she must be perfect, always do the right thing in order to please her mom, in order for her mother to love her. Now Natalie had done something her mom did not approve of, and Natalie ASSUMEd her mom no longer loved her.

Like a simple addition problem:

> Natalie ASSUMEd she had to be perfect to be loved
>
> + Natalie made a poor choice (snuck her boyfriend into her room)
>
> ———————————————————
>
> = Natalie felt unworthy of love and might as well make more mistakes!

She felt she'd already blown it! So now it didn't seem to matter: why not skip school, drink and do drugs, go clubbing past curfew, and have risky sexual encounters that were against her real principles.

Crazy how powerful it is when we ASSUME. One false inner belief about love can motivate teens and adults to make unhealthy choices: drink, do drugs, join gangs, commit crimes. Because of her ASSUMPTIONS, Natalie made more and more self-destructive choices.

Natalie wasn't the only one making false ASSUMPTIONS, however. Her mom ASSUMEd that Natalie no longer loved her either. Natalie was doing everything her mom had taught her not to. Her mom ASSUMEd Natalie must no longer care about her. Mom became angry, hurt, fearful. Her fears and ASSUMPTIONS drove her to yell, nag, scold and complain at Natalie (and we all know that when parents yell, nag, scold, and complain, it rarely makes us want to talk with them!).

There is some good news. We can CHANGE what we ASSUME!

After sharing with me, Natalie began to see that what she had ASSUMEd might not be true! She agreed to ask her mom to go to lunch or take a walk so they could have a quiet, uninterrupted conversation. Natalie got honest with her mom. She shared her fear of her mom's rejection; fear that mom was ashamed of Natalie. Natalie shared her fear that she was no longer worthy of being loved. She let her mom know she wanted and needed her support, her guidance and, most of all, her mom's acceptance.

Last I heard, they made up! Natalie is back into school, her grades are up, her softball game is back in the groove, and Natalie and her mom are talking, rather than yelling things out. Natalie, with suggestions from her mom, is making better choices, one day at a time.

I suggest we all take a moment to think about what we

may have ASSUMEd and if these ASSUMPTIONS are causing problems in our relationships with parents, siblings, friends, teachers.

MAYBE IT IS TIME TO TAKE DOWN THE WALLS, AND TALK.

• • •

Not all situations work out that well, however. Sometimes what we have ASSUMEd is somewhat true. Sometimes we can not get love from the people in our lives. I have come to realize that some people are "emotionally handicapped" and do not have the capacity to love me the way I wish they could. As a drug and alcohol abuse prevention specialist, I speak all across the United States to teens and their families, confronting the problems that alcoholism and drug addiction cause in a family.

Alcohol and drug abuse cause major problems in relationships and in sharing about feelings. For instance, if Natalie's dad had a drinking or drug addiction problem, open and honest conversations within the family might turn into angry, heated, abusive arguments. When Natalie got the courage to talk to her mom, her mother might not be able to listen with an open mind and caring heart. Her mom might be overwhelmed with her own chaotic feelings, mad at Natalie's father for his own lack of affection, love or even common courtesy in the home. Natalie's mom might feel the same shame, anger, hurt, and fear that Natalie was running from. That is the way alcohol and drugs can affect a family.

Simple addition says:

> One person in a family abusing alcohol or drugs
>
> + Lack of attention, affection, common courtesy, even violence
>
> ---
>
> = A house full of anger, loneliness, suicidal thoughts, secrets, distrust and fear

OUCH!

I have heard many teens with alcoholic or drug addicted parents speak of being told:

> "You're stupid!"
> "You'll never amount to anything!"
> even "You're a whore!"

Rarely are any of these statements true, and yet, when these teens look in the mirror, their first thoughts are:

> "I'm stupid!"
> "I'm ugly!"
> "I'm embarrassed and ashamed to be me."
> "I'm not good enough to be loved."

My goal in life is to help teens and adults recognize when there is a drinking or drug problem in their relationships. Too much pain exists in the world when we do not see this reality. Rather than ASSUME that parents do not love us, maybe the angry, abusive words and behaviors are symptoms that these parents have a serious and real problem with drugs and alcohol.

An eighth grade boy named Jason shared with me not long ago about his family. He and his dad had an argument one night over Jason's homework.

"You don't try hard enough," his dad accused.

"Dad, I try <u>hard</u>!" Jason said.

"You're a loser." his dad yelled, then stomped out and down to the liquor store.

"Dad drank a couple six packs," Jason said, hiding his eyes in shame. "He came home," Jason continued, "and yelled at my mom about what a loser I am."

Now Jason talked fast and clenched his fists. "Mom yelled back. She tried to make Dad stop swearing at me. Dad got REAL mad!! He yelled, 'You always stick up for that wimp!'…then he beat up on my MOM…." Jason paused, "and I know it was all my fault. …I don't want to live anymore."

When Jason finished, it was clear, he was talking about suicide. He did not want to feel his painful, angry, and hurting feelings any more. Thirteen-year-old Jason had ASSUMEd he was the cause of all his parents' problems: Dad's anger, Dad's drinking, Dad's hitting Mom. Truth is, Jason <u>did not cause any of it</u>. Jason was simply the child of an alcoholic, addicted parent in the middle of the disease of alcoholism and drug abuse.

Jason cannot, nor can any one else, stop a parent from drinking or from becoming out of control, violent or angry. Jason can begin to help himself, however. We talked, and Jason tried some suggestions:

1. Jason got **out of denial**. He replaced negative thoughts with positive ones:

    > "Dad has a drinking problem, and I don't cause it."

    > "Just because my dad says I'm stupid, doesn't make it so."

    > "Dad can't show me love, but I can be good to myself."

2. Jason shared with trustworthy **mentors and asked for help** from:

    - his favorite teacher

    - the school substance abuse counselor

    - caring parents of his friends

    - teen hotlines and support groups (for example: Alateen for teens with a friend or family member whose drinking bothers them   1-800-344-2666 - free and confidential)

- a sober and drug-free club at school, in the community, at church

3. Jason **set some personal policies**

- Jason decided his own life was valuable, and that he would not drink alcohol, would not do drugs, and would not hang with friends when they were using.

- Jason committed to protecting himself. When his dad's drinking scared him, he would call or go to a trusted friend's house.

- Jason changed what he ASSUMEd. Now when he looks in the mirror each morning, he starts his day by reminding himself

  "I am smart"

  "I am special!"

  "I am on purpose."

  "I am exactly the way I am supposed to be, cause 'God don't make no junk!'."

Hard as it was to talk to himself in the mirror (really, it doesn't mean your crazy!), Jason succeeded! One morning he woke up, and truly felt he was worthwhile! Our brains are like sponges. We deserve to feed our brains healthy, positive thoughts. Our thoughts impact how we feel about ourselves. How we feel about ourselves influences every one of our choices. Jason no longer feels the family problems are all his fault nor does he have to hang around and become a victim when his dad is drinking. Jason no longer feels overwhelmed by worry, hurt, anger and fear. He has begun to enjoy his life. He has found new hope! And Jason has found the real somebody to love, himself!

Whether there is or is not a problem with alcohol or drugs in our families, we can be overwhelmed by feelings of worry, hurt, loneliness, anger and fear. That is part of being human. We are all born with the full rainbow of feelings. And they all have their place in teaching us how to reach out to one another for help and support; teaching us how to be compassionate, patient, kind, and courteous — even to ourselves as we look into the mirror!

No matter what troubles or overwhelms you, I encourage you to try out these suggestions as did Jason and Natalie:

1. <u>Break through denial</u> and get informed.

2. <u>Share with trustworthy mentors</u> your thoughts and feelings. Reach out to healthy people, fellowships, and faith.

3. <u>Set personal policies</u> and replace negative thoughts with positive ones.

4. <u>Become a part of the solution</u>. For a lasting and genuine self-esteem, reach out and help others. Let your life be about service.

"Everybody can be great. Because anybody can serve. You don't have to have a college degree to serve. You don't have to make your subject and your verb agree to serve. You don't have to know the second theory of thermodynamics in physics to serve.

You only need a heart full of grace. A soul generated by love."

Dr. Martin Luther King, Jr.

The End

by
C. KEVIN WANZER

The End

by
C. KEVIN WANZER

I f you are like me, you hate the wait to see how something turns out. Well, here is a hint – like most things, this chapter concludes at the end. There, I cut to the chase. But there is a lot to be said before the end – 2,454 words, to be exact. But, who's counting? You don't need to skip to the last few words to see how this all wraps up. Instead, enjoy the journey.

It's Monday afternoon, the day after yesterday. Rainy. I am sitting at a window table in my favorite hang-out, Cornerstone Coffee on the corner of 54th and College Avenue in Indianapolis.

I'm trying to figure out what I can possibly say as a follow up to my "Don't Read This Chapter" chapter in the first *TEEN POWER*. I realize that many of you may not have read the original *TEEN POWER* so let's take a quick POP QUIZ. Please put everything on the floor and clean off your work area. A sharpened number 2 pencil is optional.

Question Number One:

Have you read the first *TEEN POWER?*

- If NO: Read paragraph A
- If YES: Read paragraph B
- If you cannot read: Skip the whole chapter
- If you can read but don't want to: Take a nap

Paragraph A:

Well, drop everything and go read *TEEN POWER* right now. It is available from any *TEEN POWER* author. I will meet you back here later.

Paragraph B:

Congratulations. Although, I hope you didn't read chapter twelve.

Now, what do I write for *TEEN POWER TOO?* I do not want to simply rehash the same message as before, especially because I do not like it when people repeat themselves. I do not like it when people repeat themselves.

I want to be inspired about what I should write. And where is there a better place than an intellectual environment surrounded by the aroma of Java beans? What can I possibly learn from being in a coffee shop?

Hmmm, life lessons from a coffee shop. How about...

- Life can be a grind: clean your filter. Or...
- Life is like drinking de-caf: what's the point? Or...
- Life is like coffee: sometimes it's sweet and sometimes it's bitter but at least it keeps you awake.

I am sorry, I kinda' got off track. I guess I am just having trouble 'espressoing' myself. I better stop before I 'mocha' fool out of myself. Maybe I should just go back home and get help from my writing partner, Dreifus.

Later, that same day:

I need to be motivated. Although I love Dreifus, he is not the ideal writing companion. He is not too inspirational. Or is he? I adopted Dreifus – by default – not too long ago when my roommate Chris moved in. Chris worked at a veterinary hospital when a small puppy was brought in that was hit by a car. The poor stray's leg needed to be amputated and Chris volunteered to become his new dad. This incredible canine lost his leg. Hence the name Dreifus. (In German, Dreifus means THREE FOOT. In English, it means DOG WHO PEES ON CARPET.) The great thing about Dreifus is that he does not know he is handicapped. He lives life as if nothing ever happened. The reason is nobody ever told him that he is different. Why? Because Dreifus does not speak English.

Dreifus lives his life as if he is the same as every other dog. (With the exception that since he only has one back leg, he does not lift his leg like most dogs to relieve himself.) Other dogs do not shun him or make little doggie jokes – that we know of. Dreifus just loves barking at non-existent doorbells, attacking cardboard cut-outs of the President and chasing a laser beam until he cannot move anymore.

He does not know what it means to give up. There are a lot of kids like that, too.

A great example of not giving up is a boy at a summer camp for children who were handicapped. Benny was about eight years old. He had freckles and hair so orange it hummed when you walked by. He was also deaf and paralyzed on his left side. So not only could he not hear, he had only one hand with which to communicate. On the first morning at camp during breakfast, Benny was trying to open his small individual cereal box. You know the type. The box is so small, you're finished after two bites. For example: Rice Krispies. There are only Snap and Crackle because there is no room for 'Pop' on the box. Benny could not open the box with just one arm, so he tackled it with a white, flimsy plastic knife. The knife would wobble and bend but could not puncture the box. The reason no adults intervened is because they wanted him to try to accomplish something on his own. Even if he failed, at least he accomplished failure – by himself. That can be a tough but important lesson to learn.

Finally, Benny bit into the box to make a hole. He sawed back and forth until the tiny cereal box opened up. The young camper had sweat dripping off his forehead, but wore an incredibly big smile. He dumped the cereal into a bowl, soaked it with milk and grabbed his spoon. Suddenly, Benny slid the bowl in front of the boy sitting next to him and slowly started to feed the cereal to him, a youngster who was completely paralyzed. This brave young man overcame his obstacles and did what most people would not even dream. He had empathy. He knew what it was like to be disadvantaged and he turned a potential negative into a positive. He was a little kid. He did what came naturally.

When you are a little kid, you don't know any better. You love others – just because. You do not care what you – or others – look like, act like or smell like. Remember the times when you used to dance and skip and sing around the house – making up songs about stuff that didn't even make sense? "I am gonna' have a sandwich, a sandwich and some noodles and cheese!" It was your very own dance – the macaroni! But as a teen, when you act that way, those nice men in white jackets take you away to that very special place…in your very own straight jacket…in your very own room made of rubber. Not that I speak from experience, um, uh, I was just speculating. Um, where was I?

When did we lose that innocence of accepting ourselves – and others – no matter what? Perhaps you have not lost it. Let's hope.

Sometimes the darkest and worst of situations can contain some of the most positive and meaningful lessons in life. Not long ago, I had the chance to visit the Holocaust Museum in Washington D.C. It was stunningly chilling –

from the piles of shoes that belonged to the victims to the tearful renditions from survivors telling their own stories on the movie screen. After the tour, I saw a big wall of white ceramic tiles filled with messages from young people from around the world. Some had drawings; others had profound statements. In studying each one – tile by tile – I came across one tile that was covered with black paint. And in fluorescent lettering, I read the words, "It shouldn't hurt to be different." The words were followed by a red teardrop as a period. I was caught up in the moment and turned to a young girl next to me, who was about 10 years old. I said to my new stranger friend, "Isn't that beautiful? Look at that tile."

The girl stared at the tile and I could hear her reading it to herself. "It sh-oo-dn't herrt to be diff-err-ent." Then she grinned at me and said, "No, Mister, it isn't beautiful. It's just true. Why don't some grown-ups seem to know that?" The girl walked away smiling.

It shouldn't hurt to be different.

Think of somebody you know who is different. I mean really different. How do you know they are different? Chances are they look, act or sound different. Many times those people are the easiest targets. Too many times people pick on others so that they do not become targets themselves. How sad. Black or white, rich or poor, short or tall, skinny or fat, straight or gay, hearing or deaf...it is all the same. Everyone is different. The fact that you chose to read this book, proves you are different. However, those who survive being targets are the ones who become role models for others. That is where you come into the picture as a teen leader.

Someone out there is watching every single step you take. (They are called stalkers.) Someone looks up to you. Why? Because you are taller. All joking aside, you are a role model, unconditionally, to at least one special person. Someone who wants to be like you.

Think of one young person in your life who you know looks up to you. On the count of three, yell out that person's name as loudly as you can. Think. Who is that person? Get ready to yell.

Ready? One...two...three...

(Insert annoying scream of someone's name here!)

I know that many of you did not actually yell the person's name. Although, if you are surrounded by strangers in public, you really missed a perfect opportunity. How many times do you actually have written permission to cause a civil disturbance? And if you get into trouble, you can simply point out this part of the book that gives permission. There is always next time. Hint, hint.

Now, that you are focused and have that one individual

who looks up to you in mind, let's move on. Before you can accept the challenge of being a positive role model for that one young person – take a look at yourself. Are you someone who you would look up to? Before you can be someone else's role model, you must be your own role model.

The bottom line is that anyone can be a role model. Even the Pillsbury Dough Boy...but he is a different type of ROLL model. The question is: Are you going to be a positive or a negative one? Think of the most positive role models in history: Martin Luther King, Abraham Lincoln, Mother Theresa, Mother Micki (my mom), Mickey Mouse...you get the idea. What do they all have in common? Well, they all have vowels in their names. They all were born with a pancreas (I assume). They all drink water. Okay, so one eats a lot of cheese and has big ears. (No offense, Mom.)

People are people. Obviously the person who looks up to you can relate to you as a person. What do you have in common? More importantly, what do you have as differences? Understand that society expects others to stand up for those who are alike. However, whenever you break your comfort zone and take a stand for someone who is 'different' the tide starts to turn. It's a wake-up call. It gets people talking. And just perhaps, it helps change someone's attitude – for the better.

Everyone starts out pretty much the same. Some take God-given positive situations and make them even better, while others take situations that most people would have given up on a long time ago – and make them magnificent opportunities. Too many times we get down and depressed about the bad times instead of seeing that it is the bad times that make the good times so great! Now, I am not suggesting that you throw a party when you wreck your car, fail a test or give your cat a bath.

(Editor's note: We at *TEEN POWER TOO* do not suggest giving your cat a bath. The fur severely sticks to your tongue.)

As Arby's Restaurant used to say: Different is Good. (That was before salmonella. Now they say, Different is a potential law suit.) Face it, appearance is just the way a person happens to appear. I can hear you now, "Ooooooooooo, that's profound, book boy." But when you look at others that way, there are no ugly people…just people who have ugly views of others. The people who degrade and put down others are the ones who really need help themselves. Now, I don't want this to become a cliché. I am not one that simply thinks that beauty comes from the inside. (If that were the case, people would be walking around with their lungs popping out and their intestines flopping around. People would say stuff like, "Nice spleen." It would give a whole new meaning to wearing your heart on your sleeve.) Perhaps, prejudging people is just a sad, but natural human trait. Or is it? I wonder how many blind people are racists? Not many.

So, what are you supposed to take from this chapter? Basically, that life is one long educational experience. It's like school – with a lot more homework. It doesn't get any easier as an adult. Like school, there are still those who make fun of others, do not share their toys, hit and scratch and never clean up after themselves. Some even get grounded and go to their rooms made of steel bars, for a very, very long time. Still others get away with things they shouldn't have done. People seem to race through life as fast as they can, sprinting towards the finish line. Once they reach it, they wish they would have walked and taken everything at a slower pace. You would think that by now adults would have learned. Some have, but many have not. Now, the tables have turned – you are the teacher. You are someone's role model. Each day we choose either to learn from each other or to ignore each other. Hopefully, this chapter has helped you develop your lesson plan for life so that you can help teach others what is pure and real by rejoicing in a life filled with differences.

Some don't learn these important life lessons – ever. Many do not learn until life's end is much to close. What a pity. It's too bad that some never grasp that people being unique is what makes the world so wonderful. If only this knowledge would come earlier in life. Then people would be able to live their lives with the knowledge that unconditional love and acceptance is all that really matters. But, you know the truth. Get out and live it. Choose your thoughts and words and deeds carefully. They're being studied closely by that young protégé you shouted earlier.

Congratulations on reaching THE END much earlier in life than many. Good luck in your continuing journey toward graduation in this worldwide school in which we all live – The University of Diversity.

The End...

...is just The Beginning.

Who Wrote What
And Why?

TEEN POWER
Too

c/o TEEN POWER
1410 Vance St. - Ste. #201
Lakewood, CO 80215
303-239-9999 fax 239-9901
800-304-ERIC
ECSpeak@aol.com
www.ericchester.com

ERIC CHESTER

Bed Bugs, The Boogie Man, and Other Myths!

Nobody likes Eric Chester. He is a lousy speaker who puts audiences to sleep with his boring school assemblies and leadership keynotes. Just look at this picture. Did he make that shirt out of an old shower curtain? His wife, Lori, married him only because her friends dared her to. His kids are embarrassed to walk through the malls with him. He's a very bad man. He never rewinds rented video tapes. He rips the tags off of mattresses. You'd be crazy to ask Eric to speak for your group. Don't do it! (Okay, go ahead...but you've been warned!)

Cordes Keynotes & Seminars
2920 Quivira
Great Bend, KS 67530
316-793-7227 fax 793-5024
800-401-6670
YOGOWYPI@aol.com

BILL D. CORDES

Not On My Watch

As a former teacher, coach and television talk show host Bill has made rekindling the love of learning for teens and adults his mission since he started speaking to teens in 1988. Bills' student and teacher programs have been featured in 26 states, Guam and Washington DC. His programs focus on character, communication, learning strategies and personal responsibility. Students and teachers appreciate his enthusiasm and creative style as he weaves together a great combination of insight, humor and excitement. Bill holds a Masters Degree in Communication and is author of the student success skills book, Class It Up! Audio cassettes and videos available.

Dr. Lewis Dodley

We All Have Rhythm...And More!

When asked what he liked most about himself, without hesitation Baba Dodley replied "that I am an ally to youth." Baba Lewis Dodley, as he is fondly and respectfully known across the country, is a gifted and thought-provoking presenter. His unique style carefully blends audience participation with real, up to date information that keeps everyone involved. With over 20 years of experience, his warm personality touches the soul of audiences large and small. He is often called upon when communities are in crisis. His keynote addressees include "Saying No! and Loving It" and "Violence and Youth; Who's in Control."

c/o Prevention & Training
by Design
24 Westerview Plaza Drive
Westerville, OH 43081
614-882-2581 fax 882-2585

Julie Evans

Sex. Drugs, 'N' Rock 'N' Roll

Definitely a one-of-a-kind female speaker, students love Julie's presentations because she's honest, direct, to the heart, and in the gut. She makes you laugh and makes you cry. And then, Julie makes you think! Whether motivating student leaders to reach beyond their horizons or inspiring entire student bodies to stay drug-free, Julie delivers an uplifting and compassionate message to over 100,000 students each year. Trained by top researchers at Cornell University, Julie is the author of "Youth Helping Youth Succeed: A Peer Mentor Curriculum." Julie lives in Oregon with her teenage daughter, Ruby, their cat, Licorice and part-time dog, Shazam.

Alive With Energy
P. O. Box 1133
Ashland, OR 97520
fax 541-488-8867
800-985-9065
motivate@mind.net

ED GERETY

The Seed

Ed received his Bachelor of Arts in Communications from the University of New Hampshire. He began speaking professionally to students in 1992. His motivational programs are shared with over 75,000 students each school year. A captivating speaker, Ed's power to reach the audience comes through his own accounts of personal experiences, including running the Boston Marathon in 1990 and 1992. His humorous and creative stories are directly related to each age group. His leadership keynotes and school assemblies inspire audiences to believe in themselves, their dreams, and to make a difference. Ed lives in Portsmouth, NH.

Gerety Presentations
55 Hanover Street
Portsmouth, NH 03801
fax 603-431-8157
800-207-2580
EVGSpeak@aol.com

PATRICK T. GRADY

Who Packs The Parachute?

Patrick, a former classroom teacher, now travels throughout North America inspiring middle and high school students, educators, organizations, civic groups, corporations and associations. In his warm and witty way, he encourages audiences to do their best in all of their endeavors.

Patrick's customized, interactive keynote addresses and workshops persuade participants to apply their talents, skills, abilities, and positive attitude to create their own future. He is an author and a producer of motivational tapes and videos.

Patrick has one wonderful wife, one beautiful daughter, two loving parents, four sisters, two brothers, nine nieces, ten nephews, two in-laws (no outlaws), one dog and a bird.

"TNT"
Today 'n Tomorrow's Enterprises
P.O. Box 471771
Charlotte, NC 28247-1771
704-541-7389 fax 543-8811
800-862-1660
ptgrady@perigee.net

MICAH JACOBSON

All's Fair...*Except Maybe Your Parents!*

With Laughter and Insight, Micah opens up the child eyes in each of us. He has been a professional speaker since 1990, and has since impacted thousands of students and schools across the country.

He has spoken and facilitated for the United Nations Environmental Program in Brazil and New York. Been a trainer for Mikhail Gorbachev's State of the World Forum, and worked with students in Russia, Israel, and Belize.

He has dropped out of planes, guided a boat down rapids, and danced in music videos; but his favorite activity remains: laughing with children.

Jacobson & Associates
1662 Lombard Street
San Fransisco, CA 94123
415-441-8377 fax 441-3913
800-97MICAH
foremicah@aol.com

BOB LENZ

Virtual Valuable Reality

"I don't want to see young people cheated out of life."

Each year Bob speaks to 100,000 youth and adults across North America with messages of hope, courage and respect. He quickly connects with his audiences through powerful stories, experiences and humor moving them from laughter to tears. The result? They leave with a message they won't soon forget.

Bob has teamed up with school districts, student councils, SADD, FHA, Beta Club, churches of all denominations and many more.

Although Bob loves speaking, his first commitment is to his wife, Carol and their five children.

LIFE Promotions
213 E. College Ave.
Appleton, WI 54911-5712
fax 414-738-5587
800-955-LIFE (5433)
BLenz777@aol.com

ELLEN MARIE

ME, The Perfect Date?

Ellen Marie is founder and president of Youth Support, Inc. a nonprofit organization that promotes sexual abstinence, leadership skills, and character development to teenagers. She has a BA in Speech Communications from St. Catherine's College in St. Paul and is completing her masters degree specializing in adolescent development. Ellen was recently the director of a crisis pregnancy center for 3 years. She has spread her message nationwide through media by being a guest on talk shows including Ricki Lake, Montel Williams, and Judge for Yourself and in numerous newspaper and radio shows. Ellen has a unique way of touching the hearts and minds of teens with a tough, but sincere message. She weaves humor with hard hitting facts to bring a realistic and straightforward message to the youth of today.

Youth Support, Inc.
3471 W. Broadway Ave. #122
Minneapolis, MN 55422
612-62-YOUTH
612-529-6884

BOBBY PETROCELLI

10 Seconds...Can Change Your Life Forever!

Bobby Petrocelli is a former teacher, guidance counselor and coach. His zest for life and sincere love for people is communicated through his message. Those who experience Bobby leave motivated by his awesome story and refreshed by his charismatic personality. As he combines his expertise and riveting personal experience, Bobby never fails to inspire, empower and encourage. He travels internationally sharing his great news to all ages, from all walks of life, in his own enthusiastic energetic and humorous way! Bobby is the author of Triumph Over Tragedy and has been featured in many magazines, television and radio programs. Bobby, his wife Suzy, and their two sons, Alec and Aron, live in Virginia.

10 Seconds, Inc.
P.O. Box 2411
Chesapeake, Va. 23327
757-547-7162(Phone & Fax)
800-547-7933
tseconds@erols.com

JeVon Thompson

Mind The Magic Wand

Since 1980 JeVon Thompson has been one of America's premier power speakers. Traveling to high schools and conferences world wide, his presentations are filled with laughter and captivating insights. He has been featured on the ABC's "All My Children" and a nationally televised Oprah Winfrey special with Michael Jordan, "Your Right To Say No." JeVon is the author of the novel *CRUTCHES* and the creator of *Waking Up From Dope* acknowledged by the White House as one of the country's most effective drug prevention videos. Please write or call for available dates.

P.O. Box 11633
Olympia, WA 98508
360-866-5500
800-525-1990
jetspeak@nwrain.com

Susie Vanderlip

The Equation For Love

Julio, the gangbanger and Susie's favorite alter-ego, says: "The real somebody to love, man...dat's YOU!"

Susie is a professional actress, dancer, speaker and prevention specialist. With contemporary music, hip hop/jazz dance, and powerful personal stories, Susie wows audiences with characters from today's real-life families in her unforgettable presentation, *LEGACY OF HOPE*. She pulls no punches in addressing alcohol and drug abuse, gangs, violence, teen pregnancy and AIDS. She reveals the true source of self-esteem, leadership and life-saving hope. Susie is known nationwide at middle schools, high schools, state and national conferences as "startlingly sincere," "a rare talent," "inspirational!"

LEGACY
4642 E. Chapman Ave #112
Orange, CA 92869
714-997-2158   fax 997-0401
LegacyHope@aol.com
http://www.expertcenter.com/
members/svanderlip

C. KEVIN WANZER

The End

Out of all the youth speakers in the United States, C. Kevin Wanzer is one that will be remembered long after the laughter. From drug education assemblies to dynamic leadership keynote addresses, Kevin electrifies his audience and leaves them thinking and smiling. Throughout the world, Kevin captivates, motivates and educates unlike anything your school or conference has ever experienced. Kevin dedicates his chapter to his wonderfully unconditional parents – Micki and Chuck. After all, if it wasn't for them, chances are Kevin would have never been born. But most importantly, Kevin dedicates this to his very best friend. And you know who you are.

P.O. Box 30384
Indianapolis, IN 46230-0384
317-253-4242
800-4.KEVIN.W
justsayha@aol.com
http://members.aol.
com/justsayha

Other
TEEN POWER
Books Available Through ChesPress

TEEN POWER *A Treasury of Solid Gold Advice for Today's Teens* from America's Top Youth Speakers, Trainers, and Authors.

PreTEEN POWER *A Treasury of Solid Gold Advice for Those Just Entering Their Teens* from America's Top Youth Speakers, Trainers, and Authors.

TEEN emPOWER *Solid Gold Advice for Those Who Teach, Lead, and Guide Teens* from America's Top Speakers and Authors in Education.